First World War
and Army of Occupation
War Diary
France, Belgium and Germany

56 DIVISION
169 Infantry Brigade,
Brigade Machine Gun Company
1 July 1916 - 28 February 1918

WO95/2963/3

The Naval & Military Press Ltd
www.nmarchive.com
Published in association with The National Archives

Published by

The Naval & Military Press Ltd

Unit 10 Ridgewood Industrial Park,

Uckfield, East Sussex,

TN22 5QE England

Tel: +44 (0) 1825 749494

www.naval-military-press.com

www.nmarchive.com

This diary has been reprinted in facsimile from the original. Any imperfections are inevitably reproduced and the quality may fall short of modern type and cartographic standards.

© Crown Copyright
Images reproduced by permission of The National Archives, London, England, 2015.

Contents

Document type	Place/Title	Date From	Date To
Heading	WO95/2963/3 1916 July-1918 Feb Brigade Machine Gun Company		
Heading	56th Division 169th Infy Bde 169th Machine Gun Coy Jly 1916-Feb 1918		
Heading	169th Brigade 56th Division 169th Brigade Machine Gun Company July 1916		
War Diary	Hebuterne	01/07/1916	02/07/1916
War Diary	Bayencourt	02/07/1916	02/07/1916
War Diary	St. Amand	03/07/1916	05/07/1916
War Diary	Fonquevillers	06/07/1916	13/07/1916
War Diary	Hannescamps	14/07/1916	31/07/1916
Miscellaneous	Battle Appendices		
Miscellaneous	O.O. Part 2		
Miscellaneous	Company Movement Orders	26/06/1916	26/06/1916
Miscellaneous	Report On The Operations Of The 169th Bde.		
Miscellaneous	Company Operation Orders	27/06/1916	27/06/1916
Miscellaneous	Report On Employment Of 169th Infantry Brigade M.G. Coy.	14/07/1916	14/07/1916
Heading	169th Brigade 56th Division 169th Machine Gun Company August 1916		
War Diary	Hannescamps	01/08/1916	20/08/1916
War Diary	St Amand	21/08/1916	21/08/1916
War Diary	Montigny	22/08/1916	22/08/1916
War Diary	Argenvillers	23/08/1916	31/08/1916
Heading	169th Brigade 56th Division 169th Brigade Machine Gun Company September 1916		
Miscellaneous	169th Infantry Brigade	01/09/1916	01/09/1916
War Diary	Argenvillers	01/09/1916	03/09/1916
War Diary	Corbie	04/09/1916	04/09/1916
War Diary	Happy Valley	05/09/1916	06/09/1916
War Diary	Hardecourt	07/09/1916	10/09/1916
War Diary	Citadel	11/09/1916	11/09/1916
War Diary	Bronfay Farm	12/09/1916	13/09/1916
War Diary	Hardecourt	14/09/1916	27/09/1916
War Diary	Meaulte	28/09/1916	29/09/1916
War Diary	Bronfay Farm	30/09/1916	30/09/1916
War Diary	Guillemont	01/10/1916	03/10/1916
War Diary	Trones Wood	04/10/1916	09/10/1916
War Diary	Citadel (N Of Bray)	10/10/1916	10/10/1916
War Diary	Picquigny	11/10/1916	21/10/1916
War Diary	Bellenfontein	22/10/1916	23/10/1916
War Diary	Lestrem	24/10/1916	27/10/1916
War Diary	Huit Maisons	28/10/1916	31/10/1916
War Diary	Neuve Chapelle	01/11/1916	30/11/1916
Map	Map		
War Diary	Merville	01/12/1916	07/12/1916
War Diary	Le Drumez	08/12/1916	01/01/1917
War Diary	Regnier Le Clerc Near Merville	02/01/1917	12/01/1917
War Diary	Laventie M5a.35.10	13/01/1917	16/01/1917
War Diary	Laventie	17/01/1917	01/03/1917

War Diary	Haverskerque	02/03/1917	02/03/1917
War Diary	Pernes	03/03/1917	03/03/1917
War Diary	Oeuf	04/03/1917	04/03/1917
War Diary	Caumont	05/03/1917	05/03/1917
War Diary	Bonnier	06/03/1917	06/03/1917
War Diary	Sus-St. Leger	07/03/1917	07/03/1917
War Diary	Simen Court	08/03/1917	12/03/1917
War Diary	Achicourt	13/03/1917	12/04/1917
War Diary	Heninel	12/04/1917	14/04/1917
War Diary	Achicourt	15/04/1917	19/04/1917
War Diary	Souastre	20/04/1917	23/04/1917
War Diary	Wanquetin	24/04/1917	25/04/1917
War Diary	Berneville	26/04/1917	27/04/1917
War Diary	H.31.c.2.9	28/04/1917	29/04/1917
War Diary	N.9.C.6.4	30/04/1917	30/04/1917
Miscellaneous	Operations 169 Machine Gun Coy	03/05/1917	03/05/1917
War Diary	N.9.c.6.4	01/05/1917	01/05/1917
War Diary	N.10.c.70.80	02/05/1917	03/05/1917
War Diary	H.31.c.5.5	04/05/1917	18/05/1917
War Diary	Duissans	19/05/1917	23/05/1917
War Diary	Agnez Lez Duissans	23/05/1917	07/06/1917
War Diary	N.7.d.2.3	08/06/1917	09/06/1917
War Diary	N.10.b.7.7	10/06/1917	30/06/1917
War Diary	Beaurains M.10. Cent	01/07/1917	02/07/1917
War Diary	Gouy	03/07/1917	03/07/1917
War Diary	Grand Rullecourt	04/07/1917	22/07/1917
War Diary	Bouquemaison	23/07/1917	23/07/1917
War Diary	Hallines	24/07/1917	24/07/1917
War Diary	Westrove	25/07/1917	31/07/1917
Heading	War Diary Of 169th Machine Gun Company From 1st August 1917 To 31st August 1917 Vol 14		
War Diary	Westrove Nr. Eperlecques	01/08/1917	01/08/1917
War Diary	Tournehem	02/08/1917	03/08/1917
War Diary	Westrove	04/08/1917	06/08/1917
War Diary	K.35.a.9.9	07/08/1917	11/08/1917
War Diary	H.29.b.9.6	12/08/1917	12/08/1917
War Diary	I.24.a.24	13/08/1917	14/08/1917
War Diary	J.13.b.4.1	15/08/1917	16/08/1917
War Diary	I.24.a.24	17/08/1917	18/08/1917
War Diary	Dickebusch	19/08/1917	19/08/1917
War Diary	K.35.a.9.9	20/08/1917	24/08/1917
War Diary	Salperwick	25/08/1917	30/08/1917
War Diary	Miraumont	31/08/1917	31/08/1917
Heading	War Diary Of 169th Machine Gun Company From 1st September 1917 To 30th September 1917 Vol 15		
War Diary	Bancourt H.36.c.0.7	01/09/1917	04/09/1917
War Diary	J.20.c.85.90	05/09/1917	30/09/1917
Heading	War Diary Of 169th Machine Gun Company From 1st October 1917 To 31st October 1917 Vol 16		
War Diary	J.20.c.8.9	01/10/1917	31/10/1917
Heading	War Diary 169th M.G. Coy November 1917 Vol 17		
War Diary	J.20.c.8.9	01/11/1917	19/11/1917
War Diary	J.16.b.50.98	20/11/1917	30/11/1917
Heading	War Diary 169th Machine Gun Company December 1917 Vol 18		
War Diary	J.20.c.8.9 (57c. N.E)	01/12/1917	02/12/1917

War Diary	Lebucquiere	03/12/1917	03/12/1917
War Diary	Berneville	04/12/1917	04/12/1917
War Diary	Anzin St Aubin	05/12/1917	06/12/1917
War Diary	B.26.b.85.30 (51.b.N.W)	07/12/1917	11/12/1917
War Diary	B.26.b.85.30	12/12/1917	31/12/1917
Heading	War Diary Of 169th Machine Gun Company For Month Of January 1918 Vol 19		
War Diary	B.26.b.8.3	01/01/1918	04/01/1918
War Diary	Anzin St Aubin	05/01/1918	05/01/1918
War Diary	La Comte	06/01/1918	31/01/1918
Heading	War Diary 169th Machine Gun Company February 1918 Vol 20		
War Diary	La Comte	01/02/1918	06/02/1918
War Diary	Anzin	07/02/1918	07/02/1918
War Diary	H.1.d.4.5	08/02/1918	28/02/1918

WO/95/2963/3

1916 July - 1916 Feb
Brigade Machine Gun Corps 3.

56TH DIVISION
169TH INFY BDE

169TH MACHINE GUN COY.
JLY 1916 - FEB 1918

169th Brigade.

56th Division.

169th BRIGADE MACHINE GUN COMPANY

JULY 1916

WAR DIARY
or
INTELLIGENCE SUMMARY

(Erase heading not required.)

Army Form C. 2118

Appendices
169th M G Coy

Place	Date	Hour	Summary of Events and Information	Remarks references to Appendices
HERCUTERNE	1-2 July		Roll appendix	See attached
BAYENCOURT	2nd		Cancelled on July 1st. ISENGALL, 2/Lt K MCFADD wounded 2/Lt R J MACKAY. O R killed	
ST AMAND	3rd 4th 5th		Coy Commander inspected Baths & Company. A/c's reinforcements to O R from M G Corps. Relieved 168th M G Coy in FONQUEVILLERS TRENCHES.	
FONQUEVILLER	6th 7th 8th		(4 O.R. M.G. Coy returned to us by orders.) Reinforcements 1 M G Corp Officer 2/Lt TAYLOR. Trenches in a bad condition, work important over.	
	9-13			
HANNESCAMPS	14		H.Q. + 2 sections moved up @ Night, relieving 1/2 6.30 Bt Rn G Cy. One was co employing up to MONCY – HANNESCAMPS road. Discovered numerous improvements well built + mostly in good condition Copied with 2/Lt Ladow Rept to whom attempted raid, My spraying D' trenches + position a Barrage upon back + Smith. 1 Rein Prisoner from M G Corp 2/Lt LECKY Reinf. posn. 12 from in div, 4 from R[d] Reserve BIENVILLERS.	
	15 16			
	17		From this post onward we shall have two – gun from firing in German lines all night.	
	18 19 20		Rather of importance from Reports being procured from each emplacement, each gun a well	
	30 31			
			R H Defence Scheme arranged	

M Raden Capt
OC 169 FR M.G. Cy.

Battle Appendices

Copies of

I   Coy: Operation Orders
       Part 1   General Information
       Part 2   Special Instructions

~~the copy of movement orders to be kept.~~

II   Report on Operation as forwarded to
       B.g.C. 169 I B.

O. O. Part 2.

1. In the forthcoming operations No 1 Section will occupy four positions in userve line
   1. in YUSSUF ST.
   1. in YORK ST
   2. in YIDDISH ST.

   No 2 Section will accompany the 2.15.R. and will receive orders from that regiment.

   N.Q. + No 3 + 4 Sects will be in Brigade reserve.

   No 4 with 2 guns in Z Lodge 1 in Main B.F.D. and 1 in Coy N.Q.

   Orders to No 3 Section later.

2. Rations will be taken up to billets 201 + 203 in Het by M.G. limbers or pack ponies, from there they will be drawn by ration parties from each Section.

   On Y day men will be issued with 1 bacon sandwich for consumption on Z day. On night of 28th tins of soup will be drawn from Coy cooks at billet 207 KEEP, on the scale of 2 tins per section and 1 tin for M.B.F.D. 1 tin for N.Q. party

3. <u>Water.</u> Petrol tins in which soup is drawn can afterwards be used for drinking water, which can be drawn from dumps in HEBUTERNE. All water used before Zero time must be fetched in these tins. So as to leave water bottles untouched. 1 Petrol can per gun not to be used for drinking purposes

The water cart men will remain with water cart at transport.

4. __Ammunition.__ There is a reserve of S.A.A. by each emplacement and at each of the belt filling dumps. Should these be exhausted they can be refilled from Bde Dumps, but Bde must be informed at once.

5. __Medical.__ Regimental Aid posts have been established at K.10.D.42. WELCOME ST. 2. K.10.D.0.8. WOOD ST. 3. K.10.C.08. WARZEL ST 4. K.9.B.8.2. YIDDISH ST.

6. __Looting.__ All ranks are warned that the most extreme disciplinary action will be taken in the case of any soldier detected looting or in possession of any article from the dead. This does not apply to anything urgently required for fighting.

7. __Armourer Sergeant.__ Sgt Sangster of L.R.B. is attached to 1 Reg th Bth. G. Coy until further orders, he will be using Billet 284 in HEBUTERNE. The Coy Armourer will receive instructions from Sgt Sangster.

8. Before marching to HEBUTERNE everything not required will be removed from limbers in order to facilitate unloading at HEBUTERNE on returning to Transport lines, Limber Corporals will replace in limbers everything that might be required.

9. Each section will take up the following :- Guns with light mountings attached M.K. IV Tripods. disappearing mount. 4. 2 gallon water tins filled. 4 Shovels short.

4 shovels Coy. to be drawn from C.Q.M.S. at Hooks Bell.
All section wire cutters. 100 sand bags. condensers P'd and
wallets. No 3 Section box parts spare.

10. _Information_. Everyone in Coy must know exactly where
the Coy H.Q. Up C.T. & Down C.T.

11. _Correspondence_. No orders maps of one lines or correspondence
must be taken further than Coy H.Q. All papers should
be burnt or left behind.

12. _Signallers_. All 5 Signallers will remain with H.Q. party
till further orders and will take up Signalling operations for
telephone & visual Signalling

13. C.C. Sects 2 + 3. will each detail 2 No. 4 for permanent
duty at main belt filling Dump. C.C. No 4 sect will detail
2 No 4 for Z hedge belt filling dump.

14. _Range takers_. C.C. 1. 3 + 4 Sections will each detail
1 range taker for H.Q. party. Senior of these (will carry
1 Box) + attend to Coy H.Q.

15. Sections in or in front of front line will communicate with
main belt filling dump whence messages will be forwarded.
Sections in or behind reserve line will communicate direct
with H.Q.

16. _Brigade time_. All watches must be checked with Bde
time both on Y day the 28th + Z day the 29th.

17. _Cooks_. 2 Cooks detailed by C.S.M. will report to
Sgt Spikes at 2 P.M. on the 28th at billet 90 of HEBUTE-
RNE KEEP. Before leaving to report for further

instructions.
18. Actual or estimated casualties will be reported as such to Coy HQ immediately.
19. No unwounded man may remain with or help back wounded men.
20. Main bomb filling dump. This will be under the charge of L/Sgt. who will be given detailed instructions.
21. H.Q. Party under charge of L/Cpl. Ward.

Company Movement Orders 26th June 1916.

1. Tomorrow (the 27) the Company will move from its present billets to bivouac in wood at D.8. near ST. AMAND. Route VIA. HENU.

2. <u>Transport & Q.M. Stores.</u>

    Transport will be packed under Bde arrangements at Camp D.14.B. + Q.M. Stores will occupy hut opposite Hut A. also in camp D.14.b.

3. <u>Order of March.</u>

    Each section will march in front of its gun limbers. S.A.A. limbers & Maltese cart will march in rear under orders of Transport Officer.

4. <u>Parade.</u>

    Company parade in road outside N.2. facing Transport lines at 7.15. P.M.

5. <u>No. 2 Section.</u>

    On arrival at camp C.C. No. 2 section will report to the Adjutant Q.W.R.

6. <u>Cleaning Billets</u>

    Weather permitting everybody will be out of billets by 6.45 P.M. tomorrow. C.C. Sections will detail parties to clean billets, which will be inspected by an Officer.

7. <u>Kits.</u>

    Officers kits + as many packs as can be carried will be put on limbers by 5.15. P.M.

6. Dress.
Marching order; haversacks on back, waterproof sheets will be carried under flap of haversacks. S.D. caps in packs.

Capt.
Commanding 169th Inf Bde M.G. Coy.

Copy.

Report on the Operations of the 169th Bde. M.G. Coy.
(night of June 30th/July 1st — afternoon July 2nd)

I. The dispositions of the Company at dawn on July 1st 1916 were as follows:—

No I. Section.

Three guns in position in or behind 48.R. + 49.R. namely at K.9.b. 85.50.
K.9.b. 85.25.
K.10.a. 1.3.

The fourth gun was in reserve in Company H.Q. at the junction of CROSS. ST. + YELLOW. ST, its battle position having been previously destroyed while occupied by 164th Bde M.G. Co.

No II Section

All 4 guns were in Y.48.S.

No III Section

All 4 guns were in Bde Reserve in HEBUTERNE.

No IV Section

2 guns were in the Z Ledge
2 guns were in HEBUTERNE.

P.T.O.

Actual Operations
No 1 Section

During the night of June 30/July 1st fire was maintained along the first three German lines, except when patrols were out.

7.20 - 7.30. Sustained fire at enemy strong points & enfilading enemy communication trenches. After this fire was chiefly directed at K.6.a. with the following exceptions.

1) 4 P.M. Enemy reported massing behind FIG-FIRM. They were dispersed.

2) About 4.30 P.M. or slightly after, enemy bombers were seen leaving EMS. They were stopped.

3) At 5.30 P.M. orders were to prepare 4 guns for fire on INDUS-FILLET. Accordingly the 4th gun was sent to a position in Y48.B. at head of old YANKEE.ST.

4) Later in the afternoon this 4th gun and one other in YIDDISH.ST. secured a good target on a large party of Germans who tried to counter attack from the Cemetery. Stretcher bearers were seen to be busy next morning removing bodies from this spot.

In making these positions, concrete & broken brick were plentifully used, & deep strong dugouts were provided, both mined & baby elephants; with the result that these four guns had no casualties in men or guns, although frequently searched for by German artillery

P.T.O.

No 2. Section

All 4 guns went forward with Q.W.R. One gun came into action in the 3rd German line on the left of the attack. Being bombed out it took up a fresh position on the German 2nd line. There it was cut off by enemy bombers & destroyed by us. One survivor returned to our lines. Two guns reached the Sunken Road (GOMMECOURT - NAMELESS FARM.) near ETCH, & from there succeeded in quietening the fire from the German 3rd Line. The after movements of these guns are extremely difficult to follow, but it is known that owing to a shortage of bombs, these guns had eventually to be destroyed to prevent capture. This also applies to the 4th gun which was kept in action for some time in either FELLOW or FELL. While these guns were continually in action, & the teams showed extreme gallantry, they obtained no good targets, & all the really effective work was done by No 1 Section from the R. line, where a system of communication by telephone & runners was employed in order to obtain information & targets from Bde H.Q.

No 3. Section

All 4 guns of this Section were in Bde H.Qware in HEBUTERNE. One dugout unfortunately received a direct hit, burying the section officer, several men & 2 guns. These guns were recovered. The remaining two guns were not brought forward till the night of the 1st/2nd.

No 4 Section

2 guns of this section were in the Z Ledge. One of these guns was kept mounted on a disappearing mounting with orders to destroy any counter attack issuing from the S.W. face of GOMMECOURT PARK. This gun received a direct hit from a heavy shell. The whole trench being practically demolished, orders were given to withdraw the remaining gun before dawn on July 22nd & to mount a gun in the R. line to cover FIG-FIRM. which was done at head of YUSSEF. ST. at dusk, the remaining guns were also brought up into positions just behind the R. line, from which they could cover No mans land & the German front line trenches. The 2nd July was employed in recovering guns ammunition & other material, which had been buried by shell fire in various positions, & on the afternoon of that day the Company was relieved by the 168th Bde M. G. Coy.

III Ammunition Supply

This is always a problem of extreme difficulty for machine gunners. Two advanced Belt filling dumps were arranged. 1) In BOYAU Trench between new YELLOW ST. & new YANKEE ST.

2) In the Z Ledge.

These would have the advantage of being near the communication trenches which were to be dug to the German positions when captured & deep dugouts were built. At the last moment the Belt filling dump in

BOYAU trench had to be handed over as a Battn report centre, & we were given a dugout at the head of new YANKEE ST. During the night of the 30/1st we moved some ammunition to this place, but the dugout would not hold it, & it was soon buried in the trench. One now was got up but No 2 Section could not get back to fetch it.

IV. <u>Communication</u>

Telephone communication was found very useful between Coy HQ. &

1) Bde HQ.
2) Belt filling dump
3) Battn report centre
4) No 1 Section guns.

It would add greatly to the efficiency of a Machine Gun Company were 2 more instruments & 4 more Sypallus added to the establishment of a Machine Gun Company

V. Finally I should like to bring to your notice the efficient manner in which the Officer Commanding No 1 Section (2nd Lt. C. V. Covington) carried out his duties. This officer had two particular difficulties to overcome.

1) There was the danger of hitting our own troops
2) There was the difficulty of ensuring accurate fire on targets on which you required fire & which were often obscured by smoke or Shell fire.

By his extremely thorough preparation & by the coolness

and ability with which he commanded his section successfully overcame these difficulties

Copy No 12

Company Operation Orders 27.6.16

Part 1. General Information.   Not to be taken beyond
                                          to Coy HQ

I. The object of the VII Corps attack is to establish itself on a line which runs approximately from our present front line - 250 yds N.E. of 16. Poplars - E. of Mamelers Farm - along ridge in K.5.a. and E.29.c. - Little Z, and thence back to our line.

II. The 46th Division attacks from the N.W. and the 56th Division from the S.W., the two divisions to meet about E.29.c. 6.0.

III. The objective of the 168th Bde is to capture FAIR TRENCH about K.11.d. 1.3, along FARM, FAME, ELBE and FELON to a point in FELL 50 yds N.W. of trench junction K.5.c. 5.2. and consolidate three strong points, viz:-
  (1) About FARMYARD, FARMER and FARM.
  (2) About ELBE between ET and FELON
  (3) About cross trenches of FELL and
      FELON with EPTE.

IV. The task of the 169th Bde will be carried out in three phases
1st Phase To capture from left of 169th Bde along FELL, FELLOW, FEUD, the CEMETERY, ECK, MAZE, ELL, and FIR, and establish 3 strong points, viz:-
  (1) near CEMETERY
  (2) At the MAZE
  (3) At S.E. corner GOMMECOURT PARK.

2nd Phase (To take place immediately after 1st Phase).
To capture EMS, ETCH, and the QUADRILATERAL in K.5.a.

3rd Phase. (To commence directly after 2nd Phase.)
To secure the cross trenches at K.5.a. y.8. where INDUS crosses FILL and FILLET, to join hands with the 46th Division along FILL and to consolidate FILLET facing E.

V. Objectives (3rd Phase)
- Right and Left Attacks - consolidation (L.R.B. + Q.V.R.)

Centre Attack - Q.W.R. - seize cross trenches at K.5.a. 4.8, join hands with 46th Division along FILL, and consolidate FILLET facing E.

As soon as possible after assault new C.Ts will be made connecting YELLOW STREET with EM3 and "E" hedge to GOMMECOURT PARK. The 2nd Londons will be in Bde Reserve and will be in Y 4 4 R 4 Y 4 8 R.

VI. All communication trenches forward of reserve line must be kept absolutely clear.

VII. The preliminary bombardment will be carried out for a period of 5 days, the attack being made on the 6th day after an intense bombardment of about one hour. (See "A")

Artillery "lifts" for 2nd Phase will be timed on the assumption that infantry will reach EM3 (between ETCH & FILLET) 25 mins after Zero time.

Artillery "lifts" for 3rd Phase will be timed on the assumption that infantry reach cross-trenches at K.5.a. 4.8. by 35 mins after Zero time.

VIII. The attack will be carried out under cover of smoke. (See B)

IX. R.E. Forward Dumps. (List of stores "C" attached showing main loads) will be made under R.E. arrangements in the open between the "Boyau de secret" and the first trench in:-

    Y44 at head of YANKEE STREET
    Y44   "   "   "   YELLOW   "
    Y48   "   "   "   YELLOW   "
    Y48   "   "   "   YOUNG   "

As soon as feasible after the assault remaining stores will be transferred under arrangements made by C.R.E. to present German front line.

X. **Headquarters**

    Brigade   in existing left Battn. H.Q.
    2nd Londons   (old) YIDDISH STREET
    L.R.B.   YIDDISH ST. & Y48R Junction
    2.L.R.   YELLOW ST. & Y44/R Junction
    2.W.R.   YANKEE ST. corner of orchard.

                       J.R. Piper
                       Captain
           Commanding 169th Inf. Bde. M.G. Co

Copy No   1. H.Q.
"   "   2. H.Q.
"   "   3. No 1 Section
"   "   4. No 1 Section
"   "   5. No 2 Section
"   "   6. No 2 Section
"   "   7. No 3 Section
"   "   8. No 3 Section
"   "   9. No 4 Section
"   "   10. No 4 Section
"   "   11. Transport Officer
"   "   12. War Diary

Copy No.

Continuation of Company Operation Orders 27.6.16

X1. **Dumps** Ammunition, rations, water have been dumped at places in Y
Sector as under :— Brigade store K.9.b. 50.51.
  Bottom of YOUNG ST.
  OLD YELLOW ST
  Junction Y & Y R
(Head YOUNG ST. — Head YELLOW ST. — Bojan de Luriel)

The dumps of ammo and water are to be kept entirely as a Brigade
reserve and are not to be used except when normal supplies are
unavailable.

X11. **First Line Transport** First line transport will be Brigaded
and come under orders of Brigade Transport Officer. Artillery
orderly will be with Brigaded Transport under orders of T.O.

Capt
Commanding 164th Bde. M.G. Co.

Copy No 1.
" " 2.
" " 3.
" " 4.
" " 5.
" " 6.
" " 7.
" " 8.
" " 9.
" " 10.
" " 11.
" " 12.

Continuation of B.M. 634.

GENERAL STAFF, 56th DIVISION.
No. SG.121/97
Date. 14/7/16

13B

O.C.D.
G.S.O.1
G.S.O.2
G.S.O.3

B.M.752

REPORT ON EMPLOYMENT OF 169th INFANTRY BRIGADE M.G. COY. on 1st July, 1916.

Night of June 30th/July 1st.
1. During the night of June 30th/July 1st six guns were employed in
   (a) Spraying Z 5 (a) and (b) and GOMMECOURT PARK and VILLAGE.
   (b) Occasional bursts of fire on MAZE, ECK, CEMETERY, and three first German lines.
   (c) Enfilading ETCH, EMS and EXE.

By 7 a.m. on July 1st.
No.1 Section.
2. Three guns of No.1 Section were in position in the Reserve Line; the battle position of the fourth gun was in Reserve, its battle position having been destroyed by shell fire.

These guns, after Zero time, were only to fire on K.6.a. unless definite targets were observed or reliable reports received as to enemy's movements.

No.2 Section.
All four guns were detailed to accompany the 1/16th London Regiment in its attack on the QUADRILATERAL.

No.3 Section.
All four guns were in Brigade Reserve East of HEBUTERNE.

No.4 Section.
Two guns were in position in "Z Hedge"
Two guns in Brigade Reserve.

3. NARRATIVE.

No.1 Section.
In accordance with orders, fire was mainly directed on K.6.a. with the following exceptions.

4 p.m.
Enemy reported massing behind FIG - FIRM. They were dispersed.

about 4.30 p.m.
or slightly after, enemy bombers were seen leaving EMS. They were stopped.

5.30 p.m.
Orders were given to prepare four guns for fire on INDUS - FILLET. Accordingly the fourth gun was sent to a position in Y 48 R at head of old YANKEE STREET. Later in the afternoon this fourth gun and one other in YIDDISH STREET secured a good target on a large party of Germans who tried to counter attack from the CEMETERY. Stretcher bearers were seen to be busy next morning removing bodies from this spot.

Gun Positions.
Four gun positions were chosen and in the short time available four strong emplacements were constructed, together with good dug-outs in the vicinity.
Situated as follows :-

No.1 Gun - Boyau in YUSSUF STREET (K.9.b.40.95).
    Dug-out mined with shaft leading down to it.
    Emplacement open with concrete front.

No.2 Gun. - Head of YORK STREET (K.9.b.85.50).
    Covered emplacement with concrete front.
    Dug-out - as No.1.

No. 3 Gun - To the right of YIDDISH STREET (K.9.b.85.25)
    Open emplacement concealed by hedge and trees.
    Dug-out sunken "Baby Elephant."

(2)

No.4 Gun - In the Parados to the right of YIDDISH STREET
(K.10.a.13)
Open emplacement.
Mined dug-out started but unfinished.

Distribution of Targets. Separate targets were issued to each gun, whenever possible in enfilade, and the fronts all overlapped. In addition several important targets were given to all guns.

Ranges. Several ranges were taken with a Barr & Stroud instrument. These agreed with ranges taken from the 1/5,000 map so for further ranges the map was used.

System of Direction. The extreme difficulty of picking up targets from description combined with the possibility of the targets being obscured by smoke and haze and, further, the obliteration of aiming marks by artillery fire, pointed to the necessity of some method other than that of taking a direct sight at a target, consequently trench mountings and elevating gears were used at Positions No.1, 2 and 3. (No.4 Position in the Parados was too open to employ a trench mounting, when the gun would have been easily visible as soon as mounted, therefore, the elevating gear and traversing dial combined with a disappearing mount were employed.) The exact bearing of the Zero line on each mounting was then ascertained.

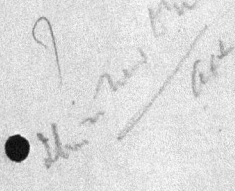

The direction of each target was then taken by compass and from the map. From this, direction could be put on a gun by laying so many degrees left or right of zero.

Elevation. Tables supplied the various angles of tangent elevation for each range, and by the formula -

$$\frac{\text{Difference in height in inches}}{\text{Number of hundreds of yards in the range.}} = \text{Angle of sight in minutes.}$$

The angle to be deducted or added to arrive at the L of quadrant elevation was arrived at from the contours.

The guns were laid level with a spirit level, and the elevating gears adjusted to zero. Necessary elevation was then given by a turn of the wheel.

Range Cards &c. Each target was given -
(a) A number for targets up to zero time.
(b) A letter for targets after zero time.
and these were marked on one large scale map, for use by Section Officer.
Each gun was issued with -
(i) A map shewing its own targets.
(a) Lines of fire upto zero time being shewn in red.
(b) " " " after " " " " in black.
(ii) Two charts shewing
(a) Target, range, direction, number of degrees left or right of zero line, elevation for targets up to zero time.
(b) Ditto. after zero time.
(iii) General orders (attached).
(iv) Fire orders (attached).

By this means, when a gun was given a target, all the Officer or N.C.O. in charge had to do was to refer to the chart and give the direction and elevation straight away.

e.g., Order received - "No.7 target".

Order given - "44 degrees left
1 degree 41 mins. up."

Communication. From Section H.Q. to Company H.Q. by telephone. To other guns by runners.

No.5 Emplacement.

During the day of 1st July the gun which should have occupied No.1 Position was moved into position in W50 just by YANKEE STREET.

It had an extensive field of fire, was directed with the others on INDUS/FILLET, and also did good work in stopping reinforcements to a German bombing party.

No.2 Section. 4. NARRATIVE

All four guns went forward with Q.W.R. One gun came into action in the third German line on the left of the attack. Being bombed out it took up a fresh position in the German second line. There it was cut off by enemy bombers and destroyed by us. One survivor returned to our lines.

Two guns reached the SUNKEN ROAD (GOMMECOURT - NAMELESS FARM) near ETCH, and from there succeeded in quietening the fire from the German third line.

The after movements of these guns are extremely difficult to follow, but it is known that owing to a shortage of bombs these guns had eventually to be destroyed to prevent capture.

This also applies to the fourth gun which was kept in action for some time in either FELLOW or FELL.

While these guns were continuously in action, and the teams shewed extreme gallantry, they obtained no good targets and all the really effective work was done by No.1 section from the R. line, where a system of communication by telephone and runners was employed in order to obtain information and targets from Brigade H.Q.

No.3 Section 5. NARRATIVE.

All four guns of this section were in Brigade Reserve in HEBUTERNE. One dug-out unfortunately received a direct hit, burying the section Officer, several men and two guns. These guns were recovered. The remaining two guns were not brought forward till the night of the 1st/2nd July.

No.4 Section 6. NARRATIVE.

Two guns of this section were in the "Z Hedge". One of these guns was kept mounted on a disappearing mounting with orders to destroy any counter attack issuing from the S.W. face of GOMMECOURT PARK. This gun received a direct hit from a heavy shell.

The whole trench being practically demolished orders were given to withdraw the remaining gun before dawn on 2nd July, and to mount a gun in the R. line to cover FIG-FIRM which was done at head of YUSSUF STREET at dusk, the remaining guns were also brought up into positions just behind the R line, from which they could cover No Man's Land and the German front line trenches.

(4)

2nd July.   7.   The 2nd July was employed in recovering guns, ammunition and other material, which had been buried by shell fire in various Positions, and on the afternoon of that day the Company was relieved by the 167th Brigade Machine Gun Company.

                                                 E. S. Coke.   Brigadier General,
                                     Commanding 169th Infantry Brigade.

14th July, 1916.

169th Brigade
56th Division.

169th MACHINE GUN COMPANY

AUGUST 1916

WAR DIARY or INTELLIGENCE SUMMARY

Army Form C. 2118

Confidential

169 M.G. Coy

Place	Date	Hour	Summary of Events and Information	Remarks and references to Appendices
HANNESCAMPS	1st	-	2 Officers Reinforcements M.G. Corps 2nd Lieut. J.B. BURNIE and 2nd Lieut. B.P. RICHARDS.	Weather rather hot
"	2nd	-	Relations. Left gun on wire at about E.11.d.1.7. them and had 3 other guns firing as well (all night)	
"	3rd	-	BIENVILLERS. Killed early in morning. Experimented in registering on enemy wire in day light, but light bad.	
"	4th	-	Here Beywith the 3rd Jean Island relief. Entertained all our day-to-in Beyrck area. Sent to that from lamp hailed.	
"	5th	-	B.G.C went round line with C.C. Transport. Line 5 new gaps - unable to work, and can hardly cross. Roped them through.	
"	6th	-	During 11th Division bombardment on our left.	
"	7th	-	Nothing doing out of the ordinary. Very hot. 5 Transport now attached from Battalions.	
"	8th	-	Hun appeared to ignore everything	
"	9th	-	Two Plat. Confronted with artillery on style. Altogether had 5 guns firing all night. Guns strafed village moving to that incessantly (at 2-4m). Item short cracks enemy MG's any heavily in retaken.	
"	10th	-		
"	11th	1.30AM	Two out one at mined dug-out emplacements completed & occupied. 2nd Indian Regiment repelled 50 Germans in front of wire. Finish on the same front with 3 guns.	
"	12th	-	Relief and began to build new emplacements in CENTRAL AVENUE.	
"	13th	-	HANNESCAMPS strafed. Suddenly searching for BENGUN.	
"	14th	-	Ditto. After 6 concentric rolls in the line were to be relieved by 146th Division	
"	15th	-	Ditto	
"	16th	-	Reps out. relieved (i.e. Sec. not sections)	
"	17th	-	Ditto	
"	18th	-	Ditto	
"	19th	-	Nothing to report	
ST. AMAND	20th	-	Handed over to 51st M.G. Co. (14th Division) marched to ST. AMAND. Relieved by 51st M.G. Co. & marched to ST. AMAND	

August   Confidential

WAR DIARY
or
INTELLIGENCE SUMMARY
(Erase heading not required.)

Army Form C. 2118

Instructions regarding War Diaries and Intelligence Summaries are contained in F.S. Regs., Part II. and the Staff Manual respectively. Title Pages will be prepared in manuscript.

Place	Date	Hour	Summary of Events and Information	Remarks and references to Appendices
HANNESCAMPS	1st	-	2 Officer Reinforcements M.G. Corps 2nd Lieut J B BURNIE and 2nd Lieut B.P. RICHARDS. Weather rather hot.	
	2nd	-	Operations. Left got on one attack E.11.d. 7.7 forward had 3 Other guns firing in all (all night)	
	3rd	-	BIENVILLERS. Still early in morning Ingersmeiled in gathering in enemy wire in day left at light load.	
	4th	-	Here Beyond the 3rd Gens. Ochrad relief. Entalyned all our day at 2 p.m. Deputation Field to dep. Bn. posts yield.	
	5th	-	B9 G not sent live with C.C. Dangerfield line 5 men each wrote the bench, and an early sign. Sighed them herself.	
	6th	-	doing at 11 Division trenches on our left	
	7th	-	Nothing doing out of the ordinary. Very hot. 5 Transfort men attached from Battalions.	
	8th	-	Men attend to "goods anything"	
	9th	-	Two Alert. Co-operated with artillery in attack altogether had 5 guns firing all night.	
	10th	-	Other stuped village indirectly that successfully (H.2-7) Fm. class enemy M.g. very penistly in attchism ft last night.	
	11th	1.30AM	Go out, I am at mined depth of placements enfield - crashed 2nd Lieutn. Peacock injured 50 Bienvere and of wire. Sent on the bring short with 3 guns	
	12th	-	Relief and began to instal new empluments in CENTRAL AVENUE.	
	13th	-	HANNESCAMPS Stayed, partially smoking. Fr BENGUN.	
	14th	-	Ditto. Riflr. C. encounter rects in the Sign as are to be relieved by 17th Division	
	15th	-	Ditto.	
	16th	-	Ditto.	
	17th	-	Ditto. Not relieved (i.e. Bn. not set over)	
	18th	-	Nothing to report	
	19th	-	Handed over to 51st R.A. Co (17th Division) marched to ST. AMAND	
ST. AMAND	20th	-	Relieved by 51st R.A. Co and marched to ST. AMAND	

WAR DIARY or ~~INTELLIGENCE SUMMARY~~

Army Form C. 2118

August   Confidential

Instructions regarding War Diaries and Intelligence Summaries are contained in F.S. Regs., Part II. and the Staff Manual respectively. Title Pages will be prepared in manuscript.

(Erase heading not required.)

Place	Date	Hour	Summary of Events and Information	Remarks and references to Appendices
ST AMAND	21st	—	Marched from ST AMAND. via GAUDIEMPRE COURTURELLE WARLUZE to Sus ST LEDGER	
MONTIGNY	22nd	—	Marched Sus ST LEDGER – IVERGNY BARLY FROHEN-LE-GRAN B. MONTIGNY. A hard march for men on short rations, but none fell out.	
ARGENVILLERS	23rd	—	Marched MONTIGNY. YURENGH YURENGHEUX HEIRMONT ARGENVILLERS. Shorter but preceeding well.	
	24th	—	Started training. ST RIQUIER area. Men in very very excellent	
	25th	—	Weather still holds good. Training should be successful	
	26th	—	Began training 10 men from 2nd London Regiment + 10 from London Rifle Brigade as Battle reserve.	
	27th	—	Manoeuvres for demonstration	
	28th	—	Heatless Rather Normanian news very welcome	
	29th	—	France very different owing to doubtful weather	
	30th	—	Ditto	
	31st	—	Nothing to report	

J.M.Adam Capt
t/o.c 169 x Bn 2 9 Coy

169th Brigade.
56th Division.

169th BRIGADE MACHINE GUN COMPANY

SEPTEMBER 1916.

To
N.2.
169th Infantry Brigade

From
169th Machine Gun Co

Herewith our War Diary for the
month of August 1916. in duplicate.

J M Baker
Captain
for 169th Machine Gun Co

MACHINE GUN COY.,
169th
No. R 248
Date 1-9-16

WAR DIARY or INTELLIGENCE SUMMARY

Army Form C. 2118

169 M.G. Coy Vol 3

September 1916

Place	Date	Hour	Summary of Events and Information	Remarks and references to Appendices
ARGENVILLERS	1		Intensive training carried on in spite of bad weather.	
"	2		Standard Brigade & departed for CORBIE.	
"	3		Company marched to St RIQUIER & entrained there for CORBIE, billeted for the night there (N. of BRAY) stayed in tents here.	
CORBIE	4		Company marched via MORLANCOURT to HAPPY VALLEY	
HAPPY VALLEY	5		Company prepared to go into the line at short notice.	
"	6		Marched to BRONFAY FARM prepared to spend night there but then proceeded via MARICOURT to HARDECOURT.	
HARDECOURT	7		Arrived at the Company H.Q. of the 1st M.G.Co at HARDECOURT just after dawn & took over them 11 guns in the line, to be in support in GORDON TRENCH.	
	8	Evening	4 guns in reserve at Coy. H.Q. 4 guns in fire support about up to relieve a section of the 168th M.G Co in LEUZE WOOD. En route the guide was killed but the officer in charge 2/Lt J. LECKIE kept control & led them to the WOOD himself. One man was killed & 3 more wounded an hours shelling on & around LEUZE WOOD & our trenches all day. LEUZE WOOD & our trenches heavily shelled. 1 man killed, 3 wounded	
	9		2/Lt D.L. CHILD wounded (subsequently died) in trench by FALFEMONT FARM. Gun disabled. Sam wounded. Gun & team in reserve sent up as reinforcements. Another gun in LEUZE WOOD destroyed by shell fire. Casualties 1 officer & man killed, 8 10 wounded.	
	10		Second gun in LEUZE WOOD destroyed by shell fire. 2.W.R marks handing attack from Eastern edge of WOOD. Casualties 1 officer (2/Lt B.P. RICHARDS) 11 O.R. Wounded. Relieved by 15th & 17th M.G Coys.	

September 1916.   Confidential Army Form C. 2118

WAR DIARY
or
INTELLIGENCE SUMMARY
(Erase heading not required.)

Instructions regarding War Diaries and Intelligence Summaries are contained in F. S. Regs., Part II. and the Staff Manual respectively. Title Pages will be prepared in manuscript.

Place	Date	Hour	Summary of Events and Information	Remarks and references to Appendices
HARDECOURT	10		Company marched back to CITADEL & lay night there in tents.	
CITADEL	11		Reorganise. One officer reinforcement arrived i/c 2/Lt. H. USHER.	
BRONFAY FARM	12		March to BRONFAY FARM & bivouac for the night there.	
	17		Proceed to HARDECOURT & take over from the 15th M.G. Coy.	
HARDECOURT	13.		Rec'd orders M.I.S.R.	
	14		1 Lieut. wood 2nd R.L.H. when reoccupied him in capture My 2nd LONDON REGT. 1 Prisoner from Bourleya., O.R. 31 killed 5 wounded	
	15		and position improved, starting point of advance.	
	16		Rec'd same M.I.S. as 9.30 pm. 1 offr reinforcement 2nd Lt. W.N. WALLIS.	
	17		1 hvy with ready to occupy idea of capture, barrage fired under orders M.G. 7ni.,	
	18		This the situation reoccupied Q.N.O.R. assembly trenches. Reinforcements 34 O.R.	
	19		O. mnt. to consolidate situation and entrenchment of M.G. Coy. we can now only keep 17 guns in action, &	
	20		4 stay with small Team.	
	21		Main M.G. line is now LEUZENAKE trench.	
	22		Main training signs of great fatigue. Discussion nothing to report.	
	23			
	24		Rec'd orders pm 23rd. W reping on high ground man aps. to pm. 2 S.A.A. & Rest guilting dumps.	
	25		at 12 noon 6 guns opened fire 9 on Northern edge of COMBLES. This fire maintained all out of 6 belts per gun per hour until.	
	26		2 AM 2nd LONDON pulled back and not to reconsider. Six rounds at 5 AM. or 10 AM LR3 captured COMBLES TRENCH, & came mi rand. 1 hvy action took up position NEQ ORCHARD in T22C (Ref GUILLEMONT battle map 1/20000). 169 Bn having been mounted at M.167 RM & lunch was drawn in support. 169 Bn Q HARDECOURT. Reinforcements 10 OR.	
	27		T Vinney moved to MEAULTE. On arrival their Capt. ECSTERNIS (INNISKILLING DRAGOONS) undwow MAC J. & command. 2 officer reinforcements 2nd Lt. H.B. NEALE, 2nd Lt. ROCHMANN.	

Sept 1916. Confidential

Army Form C. 2118

WAR DIARY
or
INTELLIGENCE SUMMARY
(Erase heading not required.)

Instructions regarding War Diaries and Intelligence Summaries are contained in F.S. Regs., Part II. and the Staff Manual respectively. Title Pages will be prepared in manuscript.

Place	Date	Hour	Summary of Events and Information	Remarks and references to Appendices
MEAULTE	28		Cleaned up.	
"	29		Marched to BRONFAY FARM where bivouacked	
BRONFAY FARM	30		Marched to GUILLEMONT & relieved 71st Lt Company in G LES BOEUFS S-SECTOR	
			Total casualties to 30th Sept 1916.	
			killed wounded * and 8 wounded	
			Officers 1* 3	
			O R 8 49	
			Totals 9 52	

J M Beaven Capt
for OC 169 M.G. Coy.

WAR DIARY or INTELLIGENCE SUMMARY

Army Form C. 2118

169th Machine Gun Coy
October 1916
Confidential — Vol 4

Place	Date	Hour	Summary of Events and Information	Remarks and references to Appendices
GUILLEMONT	1		Afternoon 2IR made a small attack to secure some position in front of LES BŒUFS, thought to be unsuccessful by the enemy. No 4 Section gave covering fire with 2 guns from the line behind LES BŒUFS. Trenches heavily shelled by enemy from 12.30 PM – 6 PM.	
	2		Enfilade action from Nos 1 + 4 entered a section of the 169th M.G.C. army to the 167th Brigade front, being extended to the left. Relief took all night owing to the congested state of the trenches + the mud. Casualties 2 O.R. wounded.	
	3		Fairly heavy shelling throughout the day. Casualties 4 O.R. wounded. Headquarters moved to BRIQUETERIE. Company relieved by 168th M.G.C. Sections relieved independently.	
	4		Company in Divisional Reserve resting in Trenches.	
THRONES WOOD	5/6		Weather unsettled. Men clean themselves, guns + equipment as far as conditions permit.	
	7		No 2 Section reports to R.F.A. for anti-aircraft duty + takes up position behind LES BŒUFS. 168th Brigade in line attack in front of LES BŒUFS with the object of capturing some apparently isolated enemy positions + in straightening our line. The attack did not succeed owing to concealed enemy machine guns. Night 2 Battns of 169th Bde. relieve 168 Bde.	
	8		L R B attack at 3.30 PM. Some effective machine gun fire, objective attained but retired at dusk owing to flanks being in the air. Nos 1 + 4 Sections in line. No 1 Section stand by to empty position in expected line of counterattack + 168th M.G. Co in the line. Casualties 1 O.R. wounded.	

WAR DIARY
or
INTELLIGENCE SUMMARY
(Erase heading not required.)

Army Form C. 2118

Instructions regarding War Diaries and Intelligence Summaries are contained in F.S. Regs., Part II. and the Staff Manual respectively. Title Pages will be prepared in manuscript.

Place	Date	Hour	Summary of Events and Information	Remarks and references to Appendices
TRONE'S WOOD	9		Garrison relieved by 4th Division. Garrison (less No 1 Detachment) moves back to CITADEL. No 1	
CITADEL (N of BRAY)	10		Detachment remaining attached to 168th M.G. Co. Company (less No 1 Detachment) marches via MEAULT to VILLE & thence p/w motorbus (under Brigade orders) via AMIENS to PICQUIGNY.	
PICQUIGNY	11		Company billetted very comfortably. By Divisional Commanders desire the men who had been on the SOMME area for 5 weeks, had no parades, & simply had to clean up & recuperate.	
	12		The Company had Physical Training.	
	15		2nd Lt Bolls brought detachment on leave to England.	
	18		Captain J.B. Butler & 2nd Lt Stubbs acting 2nd in command in his absence.	
	21		Company marched to BELLENFONTEIN with transport. Brigade HQ at HUPPY.	
BELLENFONTEIN	22		Sunday.	
	23		Transport entrained at PONT REMY at 6AM. Company at 8AM. Company en route for BERGUETTE. Arrived thereat 7.30 PM. Company moved off at 8.30 PM arriving at billeting area in L'EPINETTE PARAOIS, LESTREM at 11AM. March with men & transport the roads. Both A.S.C. wagons (rations & baggage) went into ditches & were recovered with difficulty.	
LESTREM	24		Resting in billets.	
	25	6AM	Company stood to prepared to move off at an hours notice in reserve to the line GIVENCHY GUINCHY. Senior Officers to reconnoitre the approaches there to. Received orders that Captain J.B. Butler on leave in England appointed to command 124th M.G. Co.	
	26		C.O. recommended for the field by 183rd Brigade also NEUVE CHAPELLE & the C.Q.M.S. Mr Millis etc	

WAR DIARY
or
INTELLIGENCE SUMMARY
(Erase heading not required.)

Army Form C. 2118

Instructions regarding War Diaries and Intelligence Summaries are contained in F.S. Regs., Part II. and the Staff Manual respectively. Title Pages will be prepared in manuscript.

Place	Date	Hour	Summary of Events and Information	Remarks and references to Appendices
Huit Maisons	27		Relieved the 163rd M.G. Coy. H.Q. established at HUIT MAISONS. Nos 1, 3, & 4 Sections relieved 3 sections in the line. No 2 remaining at C.H.Q. in reserve. Relief carried out in daylight with the exception of one Gun of No 3 Section. Transport bus established at C.H.Q.	
	28		Heavy rain. Situation normal + quiet.	
	29		Situation normal. Weather stormy.	
	30		Situation normal. 2nd Lt Crompton returned from leave & assumed 2 i/c command (vice Left Bates)	
	31		Baths arranged for H.Q. party & transport. No 2 Section relieved No 3 in line. 1 Blanket pm wounded. Total Casualties for month 7 O.R. WOUNDED	
			During the month the following honors were awarded to the Company:-	
			1856. Sgt. Rongots. Queen Victoria Rifles MILITARY MEDAL	
			1131. ... Macon 218.J. London Rifle Brigade do	
			762. Cpl. Porter. R.E. do	
			2623. Pte Thos G.J. Queen Victoria Rifles DIVISIONAL CARD	
			9559 Billay P.P. London Rifle Brigade do	
			1131 ... Macon 218.J. do	
			762. Cpl. Porter R.E. do	
			1990 Brown F.W. Queens Westminster Rifles do	
			2282 L/Cpl. Bayford AA. London Rifle Brigade do	

[signature] 1/11/16

Confidential Army Form C. 2118
169 M G Coy
Vol 5

WAR DIARY or INTELLIGENCE SUMMARY

(Erase heading not required.)

November 1916.

Ref Trench Map 36 S W. Edition 7b 1/20,000

Place	Date	Hour	Summary of Events and Information	Remarks and references to Appendices
NEUVE CHAPELLE	1		The Sector being below sea level, is under water and the line held by breastworks. Quiet day except for T.M. fire from both sides about S10c and in the afternoon Captain Jervis spent the day in the line reconnoitring positions & planning fresh machine gun plan of defence having regard to lateral fire in enfilade rather than frontal field of fire. 2/Lt E.E. Ewington interviewed 15th M.G. Co. on our right and recommenced emplacement at S16 a.16 in their sector. Reported that it was favourable for a gun to enfilade our front line from S.10.1 to S.10.4, was splinter proof but was probably already located by the enemy as the loophole appeared obvious. (Within the next two days this emplacement was destroyed by a minenwerfer bomb.) Just after dark 700 rounds were fired by a No.1 Section gun from M3 & C0505 on to track about S6.c.108.5 to S6.c.159.5. Heavy rain in the morning. Then the Divl. Cr., Brigadier and Capt Jervis made a tour of defences. 2/Lt Ewing fires into thigh drawn from Ordnance, to allow 1 gun to dry while others are worn. Night firing on tracks around intersection of S6.c.9.d & S6.a.9.c. S.11 a.05.15" (in conjunction with trench mortars) & S.12 a.10.30. Rounds 2400.	
	2			
	3		Morning. C/o visits trenches with Engineer Officer to arrange about the construction of battle emplacements. 2/Lt E.L. Crompton rejoins the Company from Base Hospital. Night firing on X roads and tracks about S6a, S11.6.7.4 (chosen from aeroplane photo as having the appearance of a dump.) S.12 a.13 & S.11.c.5.4. Rounds 3000. For about 1½ hours enemy machine guns fired apparently in return, as soon as a burst was fired by us the fire was made of the mark and was abandoned sometime before own operations ceased.	
	4		Captain Jervis accompanies the Brigadier round the line. 2/Lt E.M. Taylor rejoins the Company after a 16 day course at CAMIERS. Night firing. Tracks N E of BOIS de BIEZ in LA RUSSE. S.17a.8.5.60 (X roads) & S.11.b.55.45. Rounds 2750. A friendly patrol in front of one of these targets somewhat restricted the firing.	

WAR DIARY or INTELLIGENCE SUMMARY

November 1916 — Confidential — Army Form C. 2118

Place	Date	Hour	Summary of Events and Information	Remarks and references to Appendices
NEUVE CHAPELLE	5	Ref Trench map 36 S.W. Edition 7 6½/20,000	C/O accompanied Corps C.E. and Brigadier round the Corps line of defence & had been decided to retain the BRICKFIELD Emplacement, NEUVE CHAPELLE in our M.G. Defence Scheme but to put it out of use by fire along the Rue du Bois towards PORT ARTHUR instead of making field of fire, and to erect strong wire entanglements behind the road. The road had to be cleared of obstacles. This work was commenced with a party of 2 NCO's & 20 men from "A" Batt'n under 2/Lt R.L. HULME. Nightfiring the track E. of BIEZ WOOD was carried out the wind was too boisterous for accurate shooting, so firing was discontinued.	
	6		Rain fell heavily throughout the day. Night firing from midnight to 2 am at point from which it was reported enemy M.G. had been firing. During evening & after midnight bursts at trench junction S62 c 53 & X roads at S62 d 7. Work continued on RUE du BOIS with 3 NCO's and 40 men.	
	7		Very heavy rain. Captain J.B. Baker returns from leave to obtain authority to take command of 12th M.G.Co. Captain Jervis accompanies Brigade Major round night of 167th Bgde Sector on our left. Night firing. 500 rounds at houses in the SE re-entrant between 8 & 9.30 pm & 500 rounds at the LA TOURELLE cross roads between 9.30 & 10.30 pm also from dusk to 11 pm on tracks on southern corner of BOIS de BIEZ (1000 rounds). Work continued on Rue du BOIS.	
	8		Weather still boisterous. Captain J.B. Baker M.C. departed to take over command of the 12th M.G.C. Night firing. 1500 rounds were fired at the point where our T.M.S. had cut enemy wire about S50 a 24 & 1250 rounds at track leading from LA RUSSE to the wood in S66 on which movement was seen yesterday. Difficulty was experienced owing to guns sinking in emplacement. Work continued on Rue du BOIS.	

WAR DIARY or INTELLIGENCE SUMMARY

Army Form C. 2118

Confidential

November 1916

Place	Date	Hour	Summary of Events and Information	Remarks and references to Appendices
NEUVE CHAPELLE	9		Ref Trench map 36SW. Edition 7. 6"/20,000. Saw enemy's much revised scheme on both sides. Scheme withdrawn from the line. M.G. Defence Scheme now as attached sketch map divided into Anti raid defence (marked in blue) 2 guns in the front line numbered 1 & 2 3 guns in existing concrete emplacement no 3 in existing wooden emplacement. The wooden emplace- -ment today reported destroyed by the enemy T.M. So orders given for gun team to occupy a position near during the night and to be withdrawn during the day, but retained in the vicinity ready to go up if required. Main Defences (marked in yellow) 6 & 9 guns numbered 4/9 inclusive, mutual supporting, each gun being given one belt of fire as its line. No 4 at end of switch trench requires dis cut or cover for men. Owing to switch trench, difficult to combine M.G. belt of fire in belt from Brigade on our left no 5 in existing strong emplacement in NEUVE CHAPELLE (Buckfield Gun) gives a belt of fire along the road (Rue du Bois) which is being heavily wired. Nos 6 + 7 in existing concrete emplacement give a slightly plunging field of fire. No 8 will require an emplacement near and would give a belt to fill up the Rue du Bois towards Port Arthur. Rue du Bois would require clearing and could be wired. No 9 at present in open emplacement at 9 a. Might be better at 9.07 an emplace- -ment could be made for it and a line opened for a belt of fire. 3rd line 4 guns at G.H.Q. "Standing by" to occupy positions in LANSDOWNE POST (2 guns) and CURZON POST (2 guns) at moment notice. Each post has positions giving excellent crossing bands of fire in mutual support although there are no prepared emplacements. Night firing at enemy E.T.'s and tracks. Rounds 3000. Work: M.G. Mulville out working party of 60 carried on clearing out wiring Rue du BOIS and damage done by rain to emplacements repaired.	

November 1915

WAR DIARY or INTELLIGENCE SUMMARY

Army Form C. 2118

Confidential

Place	Date	Hour	Summary of Events and Information	Remarks and references to Appendices
NEUVE CHAPELLE	10		Ref. Trench Map 36SW Edition 7 G 1/20,000. Weather continued fine. C/o accompanied the acting Brig. Gen. Attenborough C.R. & round the trenches which had suffered badly by the rain. T.M's active. Night firing on enemy dumps & tracks & X roads about 36 b 05 15. In the afternoon about 1000 rounds fired into LA TOURELLE.	
	11		Continued H.M. & Stokes T.M. bombardment Several that reported by eneny lacements might firing on S.P. in wire made by T.M's. (150 rounds in bursts of 30 from front line) directed at tracks and C.T's.	
	12		Weather fine. Firing at 8 P.M. 1000 rounds on LA TOURELLE Crossroads & SIEZEK trench.	
	13		21/7th L. Turner simes from 46th M.G. Co. and takes over record in command. Gas lecture (new small box respirators) of LA GORGUE attended by 2 officers and 2 N.C.O's. Afternoon Enemy T.M's active. Our T.M's and artillery more than retaliated. Night firing about S 11 c 7 1/4 2 1/4, S11 c 4 1/2 1/2, S6a 3 1/4 1 1/2 (suspected T.M Emplacements) Rounds 1400. Emplacement at S 5 c 3 2 1/2 reported destroyed by T.M. fire.	
	14		Weather fine. Night firing about S 6b 0560 to S 6a 9070 (CT and drains). Dumps about suspected T.M.E's about S 6 a 3 1/4 1 1/4. Engineers commence emplacement at S 6 b 12 S 5 c a 2 1/2.	
	15		Afternoon Hostile T.M shelled S 5 1 & neighbourhood causing direct hits. Damage was repaired during night firing about S 6 b 2, 52 S 6 b 59 (C.T.) and S S 2 8.3. Rounds 1250 Continued strafes were carried out by T.M's to S 6 a 9 (C.T) and S S 2 8.3 Smoke was seen to be rising from a house at S 5 c 3 05 in the evening.	
	16		Weather clear. Sharp bombardment of enemy T.M's active between 5 & 6 P.M firing in the afternoon about S 11 3550 to S11 S580. S11 b 7085 to S12 a 1090 S6a 53 to S 11 c 20 56 S 11 c 10 55 & S 11 b 1-2 Communication trenches. 2000 rounds were expended.	

1875 Wt. W593/826 1,000,000 4/15. J.B.C. & A. A.D.S.S./Forms/C. 2118.

WAR DIARY or INTELLIGENCE SUMMARY

Army Form C. 2118

Month: November 1916
Classification: Confidential

Place	Date	Hour	Summary of Events and Information	Remarks and references to Appendices
NEUVE CHAPELLE	16		Sharp mutual artillery firing was carried out during the night on hostile trench & T.M. E's all S11.c 4.1, 1.2 & trenches & cross roads S11.d 7.2 & S11.d 4.2.1 also S11.c 4.5 1.5, & S12.a 6.5.6.0 (cross roads). Rounds 2,500. Enemy T.M's more active than usual. Rounds appear to be coming from Rue du Bois, from S4.c.0.5 & S4.b.0.5. 2750 rounds were fired during enemy E's S4.9.0 S6.0.0 S5.d.9.0 P.C S12.a 6.5 6.5 at M 3.4.b.0.5.0.5, S6.c.0.4, S11.d.7.5.3.0 to S11.d.4.5.10. The enemy T.M rounds were counted. S12.a 6.5.8.5 to S6.c.0.4, S11.d.7.5.3.0 to S11.d.7.5.7.0 all night on C8.S. BOIS DE BIEZ. Rounds expended 2500. Firing carried out from S9.b.20.5.5 S4.d.7.5.7.0 at night on C8.S. BOIS DE BIEZ emplacements in conjunction with any	
	19		3250 rounds fired on Railway Cross Roads dumps, trenches & T.M. emplacements.	
	20		T.M's Winnis TJ RUE DE BOIS completed FERME DE BIEZ & BOIS DE BIEZ.	
	21		2500 rounds fired in afternoon on trench railway dumps railway etc	
	22		In the afternoon 3250 rounds were fired on trench dumps railway etc.	
	23		Enemy shelling more active. 2000 rounds fired in afternoon on enemy emplacements. Usual night firing	
	24		The enemy T.M's bombardment our line in afternoon dumps tos & our emplacements	
	25		3250 rounds expended	
			a quiet day.	
	26		Company relieved by 167 M.C.C 415 M.C.C. Our anti-raid guns were not replaced by the Coy's relieving us within a few days the enemy made two raids which could have been exterminated if these guns were in position.	
	27		We march to REGNIER LE CLERC taking over there our tent billets. The transport remains at LESTREM. Near the horse standings are in progress of erection	
	28		Training is begun. a 25 yds range against a railway embankment affords facilities for firing. One section per day firing.	
	29		Training continues.	
	30		Training continues.	

J.H. Bayley Major
Lt. Capt. O.S.
for Maj 9.C.
169 M.G.C

WAR DIARY or INTELLIGENCE SUMMARY

Army Form C. 2118

169th M.G. Coy
DECEMBER 1915

MAP: Aubers 36.S.W.1, Estaires 7.C., Richebourg 36.S.W.3, Estaires 7.C., Fleurbaix 7.C.

Place	Date	Hour	Summary of Events and Information	Remarks and references to Appendices
MERVILLE LE DRUMEZ	1–7		Training continued	
	8		The Company moved into the line to the No.1 NEUVE CHAPELLE relieving 167 M.G. Coy on front extending from NEUVE CHAPELLE N roads 6.30 a 3.9. The position occupied by the 167 Coy taken over consisted of 6 guns in the front line 6 " behind the front line in strong posts. 2 " in huts held by N.R. Motor Machine Gun Battery	
	9		Company Headquarters at LE DRUMEZ N.3.C.3.1. Transport and Quartermasters stores remained at the Transport lines at LESTREM. The transport and Q.M. stores of 167 Coy (who took over our relief at MERVILLE) remained at LE DRUMEZ. This arrangement necessitated long journeys for both Company Transports. The day passed quietly in the trenches 2000 rounds were fired in the evening on enemy communication trenches.	
	10		Roads were fired on by our gunners at night. 2000 rounds being expended	
	11		Enemy mortars active with T.M's & rifle grenades during the night 2500 rounds were fired on roads & communication trenches.	
	12		750 rounds were fired at enemys tracks & roads LA RUSSIE.	
	13		2450 rounds were fired between 8pm and 1am on enemy front line trench between M.30.c.7.6 M.30.c.6.4 which had been bombarded during the whole day by our T.M's and Artillery	

Army Form C. 2118

WAR DIARY
or
INTELLIGENCE SUMMARY
(Erase heading not required.)

DECEMBER

Place	Date	Hour	Summary of Events and Information	Remarks and references to Appendices
LE DRUNEZ	14			
	15		Night firing – 700 rounds on Railway Junction at HALPE GARBL	
			Night firing 4580 rounds on trenches and tracks behind enemy lines and on Railway at M.30.d.9.b.	
	16		Night firing 4750 rounds on enemy C.T's and tracks	
	17		" " 7250 " " "	
	18		" " 3000 " " "	
	19		" " 3000 " " "	
	20			— enemy
			Night firing 3000 rds. on enemy C.T's + tracks. Hostile Machine Gun Battery (attacked) co-/ was wounded & 3 from Shell Short from Heavy Howitz T.M. bombardment of point his about D.11.c.5.8.11.	A.F.M. activity
	21	3a.m.	Billet received by 167 M.G. Coy. transport and 3.164 Machine Gun Coy grooms (M3C1.7½) totally destroyed by fire. High wind and inflammable nature of Buildings absolutely prevented its extinction. No lives lost. all live stock and civilian household effects saved.	
			Arrangements for cooperation by normal signalling between Bde observers and No 1 Section worked well. Party of enemy seen working near road M.2.F. c. 84 & fire opened. 60 feet West hang scattered but almost immediately returned. As second burst got hurriedly away 1, 2 and 3 were reported to have been hit.	
		Night 9.30–12.30	3,180 rounds on usual targets.	

WAR DIARY or INTELLIGENCE SUMMARY

Army Form C. 2118

Place	Date	Hour	Summary of Events and Information	Remarks and references to Appendices
LEDRUME			DECEMBER	
	22		111th Machine Gun Company relieve 3 nights (No 4 Section) - BRICKFIELDS, No. 6 and "13" lines. 52 Division regiment firing 1000 rounds on mural targets. Firing limited owing to No 3 Section having to reinforce Motor Machine Guns who had 2 killed and 3 wounded from T.M. bombardment. Hostile T.M's extremely active. Chiefly on our line behind MAUQUISSART & DUCKS BILL craters at 4.30 p.m. & 8.30 p.m.	
	23	12.30 a.m	Extremely heavy hostile T.M. bombardment about MAUQUISSART and DUCK'S BILL craters extending as far as MIN SK. Left took place and raiding party entered our trenches just South of MAUQUISSART CRATERS about 1 a.m. and 2 of our wounded captured. Artillery retaliated within 3 minutes. M/G's did not open fire as no raid was reported and our patrols were out. Mural vigors firing 2000 rounds only expended on a high and two strong wind rendered endeavor far too inaccurate to justify large expenditure of ammunition	

WAR DIARY or INTELLIGENCE SUMMARY

Army Form C. 2118

Place	Date	Hour	Summary of Events and Information	Remarks and references to Appendices
LEDRUMEZ	24		(The New Armoured Corps) Lst section B 193rd Coy attached to Nos 1 & 3 sections for tuition in Trench Warfare and experience. To prevent any them attempt to fraternise at Christmas elaborate programme of firing arranged between Artillery, T.M's & M.G's commencing at 7p.m. From examination of prisoners captured by 2nd London Regt. ascertained that the enemy intended to congregate at MIN du PIETRE at 9.30p.m. for Xmas festivities. No fire directed until that hour when Artillery and M/95 opened heavily. During the night 13000 rounds were fired	
	25.		Night firing 9750 rounds on enemy C.T's, roads & tracks	
	26.		" " 3250 " " " "	
	27		" " 1000 " " " "	
	28.		Firing owing to gale no firing took place owing to patrols & wiring parties being out.	do etra
	29.		Night firing 1000 rounds on enemy C.T's, roads & tracks. No wiring owing to hy't wind	
	30.		Night firing 1000 rounds on " " " "	
	31.		Night firing 2000 rounds on enemy C.T's, roads & tracks.	

For O/c. 169 Machine Gun Coy.

WAR DIARY
or
INTELLIGENCE SUMMARY

Army Form C. 2118

169 M G Coy

Oct 7

January

Place	Date	Hour	Summary of Events and Information	Remarks and references to Appendices
LE DRUMEZ	1.		The Company was relieved by the 168 Machine Gun Coy. We marched to REGNIER LE CLERC, where we took over from 159 Battle. The Strength is 12 Officers and 11 Machine Guns at REGNIER LE CLERC. We No 1 & 2 every gun in the line manned on the line by 2 Sections and teams of the relieving Company. Lieut Taylor killed by shell at MOATED GRANGE 19th January.	MOATED
REGNIER LE CLERC nr METEREN	2.		All sections paraded for gun and equipment cleaning	
	3.		All sections paraded for making sandbag mattresses. Mattresses were handed over to No 1 & No 168 Machine Gun Coy for completion.	
	4.		Company Sunday mattresses and training under Section Officers	
	5.		In the morning all sections paraded for Elementary and Company Drill. The Company had their Xmas dinner in the evening at METEREN	
	6.		Company Drill and training under Section Officers	
	7.		Sunday. Company parade for inspection by Officer Commanding in the morning.	
	8.		Nos 1 & 2. Sections parade at 7.30 am for tactics No 3 & 4 Headquarters " 8.30 No 4 Section parade at 9.15 am with guns for firing on range. No 1 & 2. " 10.30 " " " All three sections parade again at 10.45 for same work as No 1 & 2 Section 3. No 3. Section parade 9.30 a.m. No 4 Section firing on range, parade 9.30 a.m. No 1, 3 & 4. Section Parade 9.30 am for Immediate action till 10.30 am 10.30 am to 12 noon Markmanship Backs for Transport and M.T. Section in afternoon	
	9.			

WAR DIARY or INTELLIGENCE SUMMARY

Army Form C. 2118

Month: January

Place	Date	Hour	Summary of Events and Information	Remarks and references to Appendices
REGNIER LE CLERC near MERVILLE	10.		Company paraded at 9.45am for Route March.	
	11.		9.30am Physical Drill. 10.15am Elementary Drill. 11.15am cleaning Lewis's. Kit, orders to pte belts.	
	12.		14 additional men were sent to the Company today. 3 from each Battalion in the Brigade.	
			Stocking parade at 9am. all remaining matterers to be filled and shown finish cleaning and filling kits.	
			Pay parade in afternoon.	
LAVENTIE M.G.A.3150	13.		The Company relieved the 167. Machine Gun Coy, with his battery at LAVENTIE. The positions occupied by the 167. M.G.Coy, and taken over by me consisted of :-	
			4 guns in front line.	
			4 " " supports behind front line.	
			Headquarters and transport and Quartermasters Stores also the remaining 8 guns in LAVENTIE.	
			Relief completed without incident. Remainder of day quiet.	
			No firing was done during night 13/14°.	
	14.		Night firing 14/15°. on enemy communication trenches & roads. 3000 rounds	
	15.		" " 15/16°. " " " " " 7100 rounds
	16.		Situation during the day & night quiet.	
			Night firing 16/17°. on enemy communication trenches & roads. 12,250 rounds. We hope was received saying that our machine gun fire on enemy C.T.s greatly irritated up our troops, no troops have received 3 positions in German front line the effect of our machine gun fire, hence the good

WAR DIARY
or
INTELLIGENCE SUMMARY

(Erase heading not required.)

Army Form C. 2118

Place	Date	Hour	Summary of Events and Information	Remarks and references to Appendices
LAVENTIE	17.		Night firing on night 17/18. 10,110 rounds on Enemy C.T.'s, tracks & roads. Situation quiet during day & night.	
	18.		Night firing on night 18/19. 14,900 rounds on enemy C.T.'s, tracks & roads. 2 hostile M.G's replied and fired on otherwise nothing of importance occurring.	
	19.		Night firing on night 19/20. 9,800 rounds on enemy C.T's tracks and roads. Nos. 2 & 4 Relieves relieved Nos. 1 & 3 in the line & subs. Day and night quiet.	
	20.		Night firing on night 20/21. 11,250 rounds on enemy C.T's, tracks and roads. Nos 2 & 4 relieves Nos 1 & 3. Day & night very quiet.	
	21.		Day quiet. At 5.30 p.m. firing was carried out on communication trenches on one town. At 7.15 p.m. a heavy bombardment was started by the enemy and an attack made on BERTHA POST which they captured. Machine guns opened on communication trenches and area behind BERTHA POST, firing 15,250 rounds.	
	22.		Day fairly quiet. In reply to a S.O.S. signal from BERTHA POST this was opened on the S.O.S. lines. During the night 14,250 rounds were expended.	
	23.		At 10 p.m. indirect fire was carried out with a view to testing its accuracy in searching the ground in front of BERTHA POST & FLAME POST. Two Officers of the Company in FLAME POST reported aim correct and clearance over our own sufficient. During the night 14,540 rounds were fired.	
	24.		An enemy barrage was put on our posts at 7.20. All guns laid on S.O.S. lines, opened up with long bursts. Ordinary enemy fire continued throughout the night. Rounds fired 16,560.	

WAR DIARY
or
INTELLIGENCE SUMMARY
(Erase heading not required.)

Army Form C. 2118

Instructions regarding War Diaries and Intelligence Summaries are contained in F.S. Regs., Part II. and the Staff Manual respectively. Title Pages will be prepared in manuscript.

Place	Date	Hour	Summary of Events and Information	Remarks and references to Appendices
LAVENTIE	January			
	25.		Intermittent shelling of our posts by the enemy during the night. Machine gun opened in retaliation doing indirect fire in C.T's. Rounds expended. 1,710.	
	26.		C.R.A. dug out was blown up by enemy shell. 17,650 rounds fired on tracks & C.T's.	
	27.		The enemy bombarded the huts in the old German front line. During the bombardment rapid fire by machine guns was maintained and C.T.'s and tracks searched afterwards. 13,170 rounds expended. A system of repression with very depths between M.Gs. & ENFIELD Post was arranged and fire directed from the POSTS.	
	28.		A quiet day & night. Harassing indirect fire was carried out. guns firing 11,200 rounds.	
	29.		At 8.30 p.m. our Artillery bombarded BERTHA. C.T. Machine Guns cooperating with 6 minutes intense fire on the same targets. 15,500 rounds were fired.	
	30.		A quiet night. Indirect fire carried out as usual 11,500	
	31.		Execution of indirect fire was successfully accomplished. Enemy batteries about N.19.d. 9.15 were fired on several times during the day. Owing them to our 13,000 rounds were fired.	
			From 1st to 31st 216,090 rounds were expended. Casualties during the month 1 officer killed, 3 O.R. wounded.	
				H. Hockleybury Lt for O/C. 169 M.G. Coy

1875 Wt. W 593/825 1,000,000 4/15 J.B.C. & A. A.D.S.S./Forms/C. 2118.

WAR DIARY or INTELLIGENCE SUMMARY

Army Form C. 2118

169 M G Coy
Vol 8

FEBRUARY

Place	Date	Hour	Summary of Events and Information	Remarks and references to Appendices
LAYENTIE	1		He usual indirect fire was carried out during the day and night. 11.500 rounds expended.	
	2		9.500 rounds fired during day & night.	
	3		Enemy Machine Gun active during the night onwards leading from TURCOS LODGE to the RUE TILLELOI 9000 rounds fired	
	4		The day & night passed quietly. 10,000 rounds fired	
	5		Two shells and French Mortar Bombs were fired by the enemy. 9.500 rounds were fired by m.c. machine guns.	
	6		7.250 rounds were fired by m.c. machine guns.	
	7		An aeroplane passed over our lines at midnight at 10.40pm. Rifle & machine guns went up from enemy lines. 7,500 rounds expended.	
	8		The normal indirect fire was carried out on enemy C.T.'s and tracks. Two targets presented themselves during the day and were fired on with observation. 10,050 rounds expended.	
	9		7,600 rounds fired. 4 parties were fired on during the day with observation. One man seen to fall.	
	10		6,250 rounds fired. 250 rounds fired during the day with desperate observation.	
	11		7,410 " " 600 " " " " " " "	
	12		7000 " on enemy C.T.'s and tracks.	
	13		7,500 " " " " " "	
	14		8,500 " during day and night. 500 rounds fired with observation. Enemy Machine Guns more active than usual.	

Army Form C. 2118

WAR DIARY
or
INTELLIGENCE SUMMARY
(Erase heading not required.)

FEBRUARY

Instructions regarding War Diaries and Intelligence Summaries are contained in F.S. Regs., Part II. and the Staff Manual respectively. Title Pages will be prepared in manuscript.

Place	Date	Hour	Summary of Events and Information	Remarks and references to Appendices
LAVENTIE	15		7.150 rounds were fired on enemy C.T.S. and Tracks, no observation fire was possible owing to mist.	
	16		6.000 rounds fired on enemy roads, C.T.S. and Tracks, no observation fire was possible owing to heavy ground mist all day.	
	17		9.000 rounds fired during night on Enemy C.T.S. Roads & Tracks	
	18		6.750 " " " " " "	
	19		7.500 " " " " " "	
	20		The new "Anderson" mounting was used for firing 1.750 rounds. 7.000 rounds fired during the night on Enemy C.T.S. Tracks & Roads	
	21		6.500 rounds fired during the night on Enemy C.T.S. Tracks & Roads	
	22		7.000 " " " " " "	
	23		6.750 " " " " " "	
	24		7.000 rounds fired during the night on enemy Roads. C.T.S. Tracks	
	25		6.000 " " " " " "	
	26		6.100 " " " " " "	
	27		6.500 " " " " " "	
	28		11.250 rounds fired during days night. 1.250 rounds were fired during the day with observation.	
			Cannister during stormed. N.C. Rounds fired during stormed 217460	

WAR DIARY or **INTELLIGENCE SUMMARY**

Army Form C. 2118

164 M.G. Co Vol 9

Title Pages March

Place	Date	Hour	Summary of Events and Information	Remarks and references to Appendices
LAVENTIE	1		The Company was relieved by the 146th Machine Gun Coy in the line today. On relief the Company marched to MERVILLE and stayed in billets for the night at REGNIER LE CLERCQ. The Company marched to HAVERSKERQUE and stayed there the night.	
HAVERSKERQUE	2		" " PERNES " " " "	
PERNES	3		" " OEUF " " " "	
OEUF	4		" " CAUMONT " " " "	
CAUMONT	5		" " BONNIER " " " "	
BONNIER	6		" " SUS-ST-LEGER " " " "	
SUS-ST-LEGER	7		" " SIMENCOURT " " " "	
SIMENCOURT	8			
	9		A days rest	
	10		Physical drill, remainder of time occupied cleaning guns and equipment etc	
	11		Physical drill, Training with pack ponies	
	12		Physical drill, Training with pack ponies	
ACHICOURT	13		The Company marched to ACHICOURT for purpose of relief. Transport and Limber Martin Stores remain at SIMENCOURT. Company Headquarters at ACHICOURT. The Company relieved the 43rd Machine Gun Coy and had 4 of the 2nd Machine Gun Coy in the line today.	
	14		1 Gun took position 43rd M.G.Coy this was composed of 5 Guns in the Support S Ravine and 2 guns in Defences of ACH COURT	

WAR DIARY
or
INTELLIGENCE SUMMARY
(Erase heading not required.)

Army Form C. 2118

Title Pages **March**

Place	Date	Hour	Summary of Events and Information	Remarks and references to Appendices
ACHICOURT	14	contd	3 Guns taken away from part of 21st Machine Gun Coy in ACHICOURT Defences.	
	15		2000 rounds were fired during the night on Enemy C.T's Roads & Dumps	
	16		1,500 " " " "	
	17		3,250 " " " "	
	18		4,000 " " " "	
			All guns withdrawn from ACHICOURT Defences. 2 Guns of N.º Section take up positions in Enemy 2nd line behind BEAURAINS.	
	19		Part of Transport come today to ACHICOURT from SIMENCOURT. Number of Section awaited positions in old British Line and took up positions in Enemy new 2nd line.	
	20		Two new Machine Gun Emplacements made in new position, another one almost completed.	
	21		Heavy shelling all night by the enemy on road in M.17.C. Enemy shelled continuously all night in the vicinity of 3 forward gun about M.11.B. C & D.	
	22		Enemy shelled the vicinity of emplacements at M.11.B.6.0.70. during the day. 2 Emplacements unfinished, another commenced, also 2 shelter erected	
	23		150 rounds were fired during past 17th night on Enemy M.G.n TELEGRAPH HILL. General work of improving etc continued	
	24		Shelling intensely generally last night. Two pair of gun legs of the enemy coming from Enemy line in direction of TELEGRAPH HILL Enemy sent a great number of White Verey Shots 20 Yds in front of gun at M.17.B.6.F.70. General work of improving continued	

WAR DIARY or INTELLIGENCE SUMMARY

Army Form C. 2118

(Erase heading not required.)

Place	Date	Hour	Summary of Events and Information	Remarks and references to Appendices
ACHICOURT	27.		Enemy shelled intermittently all night. Also PRUESSEN WEG. Today between 2pm and 4pm with light shells. Two emplacements erm course of construction at M.D.6.T.80. 60 rounds fired from position at M.D.6.T. at enemy aeroplane.	
	28.		100 Rounds fired on hostile Aeroplane which returned to its own lines. Hostile artillery active all night. Hostile Machine Guns comparatively quiet. Trenches in very bad condition as result of bad weather.	
	29.		Fine was brought to bear on Enemy observed in VOSGES behind TELEGRAPH HILL 210 rounds fired. No apparent result noted.	
	28.		During the night several shelling of entrances to BED'D HAIRPINS and PRUESSEN WEG. 1500 rounds were fired on gaps between our at N. 13.C.I.T, N. 19.2. 25.N.T. and N. 24.B.2.3. Also on workings party in VALLEY behind TELEGRAPH HILL. Weather very bad. Enemy hostile shelling of BEAURAINS VILLAGE. No 4. Section relieved hostile Machine Guns not so active as usual.	
	29.		No 2. Section in the line.	
	30.			
	31.		No 1. Section on returning from fatigue in the line were hit by a shell in the square ACHICOURT at 7am. Casualties 2 killed 7 wounded. No 3 Section was relieved by 167th Machine gun Coy in the line today "160". " " ". " " " "	

Total Casualties: Officers nil. Other Ranks 2 killed [illegible]

[Signed]
Lt. 169. Machine Gun Coy.

MAP. NEUVILLE VITASSE.
51.B.S.W.1.

169 M.G. Coy
Vol 10

WAR DIARY
or
INTELLIGENCE SUMMARY

APRIL

Place	Date	Hour	Summary of Events and Information	Remarks and references to Appendices
ACHICOURT	1.		The Company remains at ACHICOURT. The day is spent in cleaning guns equipment etc.	
	2.		The 169 Infantry Brigade went to MONCHIET the Company remains in ACHICOURT. Sections practised coming into action with pack mules, signallers, runners, and rangefinders being employed.	
	3.		Sections practised coming into action with pack mules etc as on the 2nd. One Section was working on the line during the night.	
	4.		Sections practised coming into action with pack mules etc as on the 2nd. One Section was working on the line during the night.	
	5.		Same as on the 2nd. One Section working in the line during the night carrying stores etc in preparation for the attack.	
	6.		Practiced in loading pack mules etc one section carrying stores to the line during the night in preparation for the attack. Three parts the teams at ACHICOURT stood during the night by enemy. One other rank wounded	
	7.		The enemy shelled the vicinity of the guns at ACHICOURT nearly all day. Several teams toward with shells were up that fire and the Belts had to be vacated the front of Headquarters was blown in and the whole of the material damaged. All guns were now the commanding Officer was slightly wounded and also one other rank.	
	8.		No 1 and 2 Sections went into the line and took up positions at firsts on GRUNDHERR WEG approximately at M.23.B.7.7.	

WAR DIARY or INTELLIGENCE SUMMARY

Army Form C. 2118

Place	Date	Hour	Summary of Events and Information	Remarks and references to Appendices
BOISLEUX S.	8.		Nos 3 and 4 Sections were in reserve and took up positions in assembly area at M.30.a.80. Nos 1 and 2 Sections go forward and give support at M.23.B.7. All reserve rations I.R.R. etc at Company HQ. at M.29.B.7.	
	9.		The attack takes place and NEUVILLE VITASSE is taken. Nos 1 and 2 Sections go forward and give support to the 30th Division advancing on our right.	
	10.		Slightly quiet in consolidating. Ordered this support was given by Nos 1 and 2 Sections during attack on the EGG. 1 O.R. wounded.	
	11.		Nos 1 and 2 Sections come down from ACHICOURT. Nos 3 and 4 Sections move up the line from reserve to relieve the 167. Machine Gun Company. Brigade HQ moves to NEUVIELLE VITASSE.	
	12.		WANCOURT and HENINEL taken in the morning. All Sections and Company HQ move to outskirts of HENINEL in sunken road. No 4 Section gun in front line. Nos 1, 2 & 3 Sections remain in reserve at Company HQ. Transport and Quartermaster Stores remain in the open.	
HENINEL	13.		behind NEUVILLE VITASSE and have in the open. 1 Officer and 3 O.R. wounded. 1 Machine gun temporarily out of action owing to friend barrel casing.	
	14.		Nos 1, 2 & 3 Sections go in front line to give overhead fire for LR attack that took place at 5:30 a.m. The attack failed owing to divisions on right and left failing to obtain their objectives. 5 O.R. wounded. 1 Gun temporarily out of action owing to broken connecting rod. All Sections move out of the line and go to Transport lines behind NEUVILLE VITASSE.	

WAR DIARY or **INTELLIGENCE SUMMARY**
(Erase heading not required.)

Army Form C. 2118

Place	Date	Hour	Summary of Events and Information	Remarks and references to Appendices
ACHICOURT	15.		All sections move to ACHICOURT also Lug H.2. and Transport and Quarter masters stores	
	16.		Day spent in cleaning gun equipment etc.	
	17.			
	18.			
SOUASTRE	19. 20.		General training commenced. Company continued Transport move out from ACHICOURT, entrained on the main ARRAS DOULLENS road and proceed to POUASTRE for a rest. Transport arrived in a few hours before the Company.	
	21.		Running drill in morning from 7.20 - 7.45.	
	22.		Ordinary machine gun training under section Officers.	
	23.		Sunday. The day is free. 1 Officer and N other ranks reinforcements.	
			Running drill from 7.20 - 7.45 am. Inspection of new draft by the C.O. also inspection of all N.C.O's with exception of Sergeants. Ordinary machine gun training under section Officers.	
WARQUETIN	24.		Running and training as above. Urgent telegram received at 11.am to be ready to move at 2 p.m. Company march from POUASTRE to WARQUETIN and stay the night.	
	25.		Company remain at WARQUETIN	
BERNEVILLE	26.		Company march from WARQUETIN to BERNEVILLE and stay the night.	
	27.		Company remain at BERNEVILLE for the day.	
H.31.C.2.9	28.		Company march to Beyond ARRAS and burin in the 9 p.m. at H.31.C.2.9 where we remain in support. 8 a.m. Stores remain in ARRAS.	
	29.		2 Guns of No.3 Section go in to the lit alloted by No.4 Section and when this is completed Gun Crews Nº 1, 2: 3: & 4. of No.3 Section reply as N°.3. position taken up as N°.3. position H.Q. N° 2. E.F.7. and gun position A. and O.19.a.1.85. 7.º 4. Section at N°. 2 1.º 4. N°. 2. E.F.9. and gun Nº O.15.b.1.5. Nº. 18. C.8.4. and O.13. b.1.5.	

1875 Wt. W593/826 1,000,000 4/15 J.B.C. & A. A.D.S.S./Forms/C. 2118.

WAR DIARY
or
INTELLIGENCE SUMMARY
(Erase heading not required.)

Army Form C. 2118

Place	Date	Hour	Summary of Events and Information	Remarks and references to Appendices
N.9.c.6.4.	20.		The remainder of the Company moved up to in trenches two N.9.c.6.4.6. N.19.D.1.5. Transport remains at H.31.c.r.9. The Offr. Pattn. Coy. Bring up Major E.C.S. JERVIS although wounded remained & this Group and takes over command of the Divisional M.G. Coy. C.193rd Inf. Bde.) Hodge 193rd Infy Coy takes over Captain B.B. ROMSBY takes over command of the 56th Group. The 170 & 171st Coy Company E.C.S. JERVIS temporarily promoted to Captain. 2nd Lt. H. USHER temporary Captain is in command of Company. Casualties for the month Killed 6. Other ranks. Wounded Offrs 1. Other Ranks. 15.	

Trimmer LG
2/Lt. 169. Machine Gun Company.

1. May. 1917.

War Diary

3rd May. 1917. Continued.

Operations 169. Machine Gun Coy.

After our attack on left flank failing enemy sought to reinforce his front line in TOOL TRENCH and large numbers were seen concentrating near O.8 Central probably for counter-attack.

The 2 forward Machine Guns fired on all these parties and prevented any possibility of counter attack developing from left.

Had counter attack developed from left it would have meant complete cutting off of all our troops in advance of CAVALRY FARM.

MAP. ETERPIGNY
Sheet 51 b N.W. N.E and S.W.

WAR DIARY or **INTELLIGENCE SUMMARY**
(Erase heading not required.)

Army Form C. 2118

169 M G Coy
Vol XI

May 1917

Place	Date	Hour	Summary of Events and Information	Remarks and references to Appendices
N.9.c.6.4.	1.		A practice barrage is put up by our artillery in early morning. Enemy sent over shrapnel gas shells. Our machine guns are now situated thus. 2 guns in O.13.a. F.S. 2 guns in O.19.a. 30.90. and 2 guns in N.9.C.64. anti-aircraft purposes. The remaining guns at H.Q. of N.9.C.6.4. The 193rd Bty carry across 2 of our guns in evening. Evacuation by Cable Chaufie ok. Ranks. 3 Killed 4 Wounded.	
N.10.C.70.50.	2.		No 3 Section (4 guns) move up to dismounting trench dugout at O.13.13 from TANK TRENCH. No 2 and all remaining guns move up to forward position in N.10.C.70.50. in NOVA SCOTIA TRENCH.	
	3.	3.45 a.m	No 3 Section go forward partly led up by Lieut. Met his from Zero hour, position of CAVALRY FARM in ARRAS CAMBRAI ROAD. also from Cavalry Enemy saw No 3 Sec approach the Kol a dense L grate of material at 20 yards led by a fast. The enemy chiefly Offrs., owing to the enemy escaped on artillery barrage. The machine guns eventually got beyond CAVALRY FARM. 2 guns are turned with them and securing 1000 field, the enemy eventually puts up White Flag and surrender 25 strong to C. Wallis (No 3 Section) in charge gds. 2 guns shell put in same many good targets presented themselves and were affectively dealt with, among the enemy seen to fall as result from M.G. fire. Guns were eventually withdrawn. 1 Gun in O.14.a.0.8. checking along front of TOOL TRENCHES. 1 Gun along HILLSIDE WORK. and to gun forming cut of to west Counter attack observed to break through his held by infantry of O.B.A.4.J. Infantry in sight and left having failed to get through Brigade order me to retire to original line in evening. Casualties for the day. 1 Offr Wounded. 13 OR wounded. One machine gun was destroyed by Shell fire.	
W.31.c.r.5	4.		Company was relieved by 168 M G Coy. Company moves to Retakes of LE TILLOY at W.31.c.5.5. where we hung out in the open.	
	5.			
	6.			
	7.			
	8.			
	9.			
	10.		Company resting and doing minor work of cleaning shells etc. One section practising emplating shell hole. Company continues easy training also cleaning shell poles etc.	

WAR DIARY
or
INTELLIGENCE SUMMARY

(Erase heading not required.)

May continued

Army Form C. 2118

Place	Date	Hour	Summary of Events and Information	Remarks and references to Appendices
H.31.C.5.5.	11.		Training under Section Officers and coloring operations	
	12.		" " " " " " "	
	13.		" " " " " " "	
	14.		" " " " " " "	
	15.		Training under Section Officers and coloring operations. 1 Officer and N.C.O. per Company from the Infantry Battalions (2nd London Regt and Devon) commence a 5 days course, given by this company on the use of the German machine gun.	
	16.		Training etc as on the 15th	
	17.		Training etc as on the 15th	
	18.		Training etc as on the 15th	
	19.		Training etc as on the 15th	
DUISSANS	19.		Company moved from H.31.C.5.5. at 10 a.m. and proceeded to DUISSANS	
	20.		General machine gun training in morning. Voluntary swimming in afternoon. Course to Infantry on German Machine Gun continued as on 15th	
	21.		— do —	
	22.		Parade cancelled owing to heavy rain. Course to Infantry on German machine gun continued as on 15th.	
	23.		Early morning swimming and general training continued	
AGNEZ LEZ DUISSANS	24.		Company move to AGNEZ LEZ DUISSANS.	
	25.		Early morning swimming and general training continued	
	26.		Early morning swimming. Inspection by G.O.C. 56. Division	
	27.		Sunday. Church Parade	
	28.		Early morning swimming. Tank saddlery training	
	29.		Early morning swimming. Review practice	
	30.		all N.C.O's were instructed under a Regiat maps instructor detailed by Brigade	

Army Form C. 2118

WAR DIARY
or
INTELLIGENCE SUMMARY

May Continued (Erase heading not required.)

Place	Date	Hour	Summary of Events and Information	Remarks and references to Appendices
AGNEZ LEZ DUISANS	31.		Usual Drumming and General training continued. Mentioned in Despatches. Lieut J. Leski and 7146 L. Cpl S.M. King J.W. Casualties for the month. Killed 1 Other Ranks. Wounded 2 Officers 33 Other Ranks. Drinn Kee Lt Lieut 169 Machine Gun Coy 2/c 169 Machine Gun Coy.	

Maps LENS 11
FRANCE 57 B.S.W.

169 M.G. Coy

Vol 72

WAR DIARY
or
INTELLIGENCE SUMMARY
(Erase heading not required.)

Army Form C. 2118

Instructions regarding War Diaries and Intelligence Summaries are contained in F.S. Regs., Part II. and the Staff Manual respectively. Title Pages will be prepared in manuscript.

Place	Date JUNE	Hour	Summary of Events and Information	Remarks and references to Appendices
AGNEZ LEZ DUISANS.	1 to 7.		General Training continued, composed of Swimming, Mechanism, Stoppages, Revolver Practice, Route-marching etc.	
N.7.d.2.3	8.		Company moved to N.7.d.2.3. Transport and Q.M. Stores near Beaurains taking over from 42nd M.G. Coy.	
	9.		Company H.Q. of H1 at M.G. Coy. were taken over at N.7.d.2.3. No.3 Section relieved 4 guns of H1 sec M.G. Coy. near Wancourt at positions N.2.b.8.4. N.22.a.95.25. N.16.b.3.2. and N.23.b.6.0.	
N.10.b.7.7.	10		Company moved to Advanced H.Q. at N.10. Section 3 relieved by 193 M.G.C.	
	11		Distribution of Sections Section 1 - one team in reserve at Company H.Q. - remaining three teams in "CORPS LINES" at N.11.d.2.3. N.12.c.4.4. N.12.c.3.6. Section 2. with subsection of 193 M.G. Coy. six guns at O.20.c.60.45. O.20.c.9.9. O.19.b.85.45. O.19.cent. O.9.a.9.8. O.19.a.95.60. Section 3. in reserve in WANCOURT LINE at N.10.a.95.30. Section 4. 2 guns in shell holes in front of RAKE TRENCH at O.13.b.3.6. O.13.b.3.7. and 2 guns in shell holes in front of SPADE TRENCH at O.7.d.4.1 and O.7.d.4.2.	

Army Form C. 2118

WAR DIARY
or
INTELLIGENCE SUMMARY
(Erase heading not required.)

Instructions regarding War Diaries and Intelligence Summaries are contained in F. S. Regs, Part II. and the Staff Manual respectively. Title Pages will be prepared in manuscript.

Place	Date	Hour	Summary of Events and Information	Remarks and references to Appendices
	12		Quiet night 11/12 - enemy aircraft over gun positions in front of WANCOURT continuously from 2.30 a.m. to 7.30 a.m. - emplacements, entrances, and trenches deepened, and ammunition recesses made - alternate positions dug. No. 2 gun. No. 2 section moved from O.20.C.9.9 to O.20.C. 90.45. additional team of 193 M.G. Coy. at N.24.d. 85.40. 4/14:13 Pte Johnson St. wounded in hand by shell fragment while acting as Section 4 runner. Orders issued by O.C. regarding operations in conjunction with Brigade on left.	
	13.		Emplacements improved, aiming marks put out, and bearings taken for operations tomorrow.	
	14	Zero 7.20 a.m.	Infantry attack on HOOK and LONG TRENCHES.	
		7.21½ a.m.	Group "A" of 4 guns under Lt USHER near O.19.b.9.4 opened intense fire enfilading LANYARD TRENCH between O.15.a. 0.6 and O.9.C. 40.25. Group "B" of 4 guns under Lt WALLIS, between O.9.d. 48.20 and O.9.d. 50.30 opened intense barrage fire on BOIS DU VERT, STIRRUP LANE and SPUR TRENCH.	
		7.25 a.m.	Party of 10-15 Germans seen to leave LANYARD TRENCH near ARRAS-CAMBRAI RD.	
		7.31½ a.m.	Slow searching fire opened by both groups on same lines and attention paid to dangerous spots.	

WAR DIARY
or
INTELLIGENCE SUMMARY
(Erase heading not required.)

Army Form C. 2118

Instructions regarding War Diaries and Intelligence Summaries are contained in F.S. Regs., Part II. and the Staff Manual respectively. Title Pages will be prepared in manuscript.

Place	Date	Hour	Summary of Events and Information	Remarks and references to Appendices
	14 Cont.	9.20 a.m.	Firing ceased and guns laid on S.O.S. lines.	
		5.30 p.m.	ROUNDS FIRED from 4.21½ a.m. to 9.20 a.m. - Group "A" - 11,000 Group "B" - 10,000 Enemy counter attack on left - both groups opened heavy barrage fire on S.O.S. lines in accordance with instructions.	
	15.	5 a.m.	Company H.Q. removed from N.10.b.7.7. to N.10.a.95.30.	
	16	2.20 a.m.	At 10 p.m. on 15th six guns opened long range harassing fire on tracks in O.9. This was continued until 2.20 a.m. when enemy put down a barrage N. of ARRAS-CAMBRAI Rd. These six guns then returned to their S.O.S. lines of fire and increased their rate.	
		3.30 a.m.	Firing slackened at 3 a.m. and ceased at 3.30 a.m. Rounds fired:- 6,000	
		9.30 a.m.	Section 2 relieved by 193 M.G. Coy. The following message was received from H.Q. 3rd Division. "Very many thanks for your co-operation in operations. Your assistance materially contributed to our success."	
	17.		No.1 Section relieved by No.3 Section in CORPS LINE - No.4 section relieved by No.1. Section in front line system. No.4 Section returned to Company H.Q.	

1875 Wt. W593/826 1,000,000 4/15 J.B.C. & A. A.D.S.S./Forms/C.2118.

Army Form C. 2118

WAR DIARY
or
INTELLIGENCE SUMMARY
(Erase heading not required.)

Instructions regarding War Diaries and Intelligence Summaries are contained in F.S. Regs., Part II. and the Staff Manual respectively. Title Pages will be prepared in manuscript.

Place	Date	Hour	Summary of Events and Information	Remarks and references to Appendices
	17 Cont.	5 a.m. to 12 n.n	Over 150 shells fell in neighbourhood of Section H.Q. at N.11.d.2.3.	
	18.		During night 17/18 enemy shelled vicinity of positions in CORPS LINE with gas shells.	
		1 a.m to 2 a.m.	Both guns in SPADE TRENCH fired in answer to S.O.S. signals. Number of rounds fired: 1000.	
	19.		Situation very quiet - no firing done.	
	20.		Situation again very quiet. Sections 1 and 3 relieved by 168 M.G. Coy.	
	20/21.		All sections moved to Coy. H.Q. at M.10. central.	
	22		Gun and gun kit cleaning under Sectional arrangements.	
	23.		Church Parades.	
	24 25		Gun and gun kit cleaning - elementary Gun Drill under Section officers	
			General training, including Company Drill, Saluting Drill, and Aiming Instruction. Salvage during afternoons.	
			CASUALTIES for the month :- 1 O.R. wounded	

for O.C. 169 Machine Gun Company.

1875. Wt. W.593/826 1,000,000 4/15. J.B.C. & A. A'D.S.S./Forms/C. 2118.

No. 169 MACHINE GUN COMPANY. 30
No. MG 91
Date 30/6/17

169 MRC Vol 13

Maps. FRANCE { 51.B.s.w. / 51.C.

WAR DIARY or INTELLIGENCE SUMMARY

Army Form C. 2118

(Erase heading not required.)

JULY 1917.

Place	Date	Hour	Summary of Events and Information	Remarks and references to Appendices
BEAURAINS. M.10.cent:	JULY 1.		Church Parade.	
	2.	2 p.m.	Company moved to GOUY EN ARTOIS via AGNY, WAILLY, BEAUMETZ, and MONCHIET.	
GOUY.	3.	"	" " GRAND RULLECOURT via FOSSEUX and BARLY.	
GRAND RULLECOURT.	4 } 5 }	-	Company training including Physical Drill, Company Drill, and general Machine Gun Training.	
	6.	11.a.m	Rehearsal of Church Parade in Chateau Grounds in preparation for visit of His Majesty the King on 8th. inst. Six guns of this Company were detailed by Third Army for Anti Aircraft defence purposes at BAVINCOURT. Disposition of guns. 2 M.G. at P. 35. d. 0.6. 2 M.G. " P. 34. c. 6.4. 2 M.G. " P. 35. a 40.95 H.Q. situated at P. 35. d. 0.6. All guns were connected by telephone direct with O.C. Anti Aircraft Defences, Third Army.	
		3 p.m.	Party composed of 3 officers, 7 gun teams, 3 signallers, and 3 cooks proceeded to take up above positions.	

Army Form C. 2118

WAR DIARY
or
INTELLIGENCE SUMMARY
(Erase heading not required.)

Instructions regarding War Diaries and Intelligence Summaries are contained in F. S. Regs., Part II. and the Staff Manual respectively. Title Pages will be prepared in manuscript.

JULY.

Place	Date	Hour	Summary of Events and Information	Remarks and references to Appendices
GRAND RULLECOURT.	7.		General Company Training.	
	8.		Church Parade abandoned owing to inclemency of weather.	
	9.		43 officers and O.R. were inoculated. T.A.B. ½ cc.	
	10.		Inoculated officers and men excused duty for 48 hrs. from time of inoculation. No parades were held.	
	11.		Brigade Route March. MAP. 51.c. Starting Point. Cross Roads. O. 21.a. 3.3. Cross Roads. O. 21.a. 3.3. - Road Junction in WARLUZEL O.24.c.3.0. - Route. Cross Roads. O. 20.a.6.0. - thence shortest route to billets.	
	12. 13.		Range Exercises.	
	14.		Route March. Starting Point. O.9.a.4.9 Route: GRAND RULLECOURT - H.34.c.5.3. - N.24.a. cent. - D.19.a.2.4. - GRAND RULLECOURT.	
	15.		Inspection of Revolvers.	
	16.		Revolver practice during forenoon. Brigade Sports during afternoon.	
	17.		Parade under Section Officers - Brigade Sports during afternoon.	
	18.		Gas appliances inspected. Whole Company inoculated.	
	19.		No parades.	

WAR DIARY
or
INTELLIGENCE SUMMARY
(Erase heading not required.)

Army Form C. 2118

Place	Date	Hour	Summary of Events and Information	Remarks and references to Appendices
GRAND RULLECOURT	20		Half section range exercises. Remainder tactical scheme with 14 guns. Parade under Section Officers during afternoon.	
	21.		Cleaning and packing of limbers.	
	22.	8.30 a.m.	Company moved from GRAND RULLECOURT to BOUQUEMAISON via SUS ST LEGER, IVERGNY, and LE SOUICH.	
BOUQUEMAISON	23.		Company drill in forenoon	
		6.53 p.m.	Company entrained for WIZERNES, arriving at midnight. On detrainment company marched to HALLINES and billeted for the night.	
HALLINES.	24.		Company moved to WESTROVE in EPERLECQUES area, near ST. OMER.	
WESTROVE	25.		General Machine Gun Training, cleaning guns and ammunition, and repacking limbers.	
	26		Physical Training. Squad Drill, and M.G. training during forenoon. Demonstrations and driving drill during afternoon.	
	27.	9 a.m. to 4 p.m.	Tactical Schemes.	
	28.		General Company Training with route march in afternoon for those whose inoculation was complete. Remainder inoculated.	

Army Form C. 2118

WAR DIARY
or
INTELLIGENCE SUMMARY
(Erase heading not required.)

Instructions regarding War Diaries and Intelligence Summaries are contained in F.S. Regs., Part II. and the Staff Manual respectively. Title Pages will be prepared in manuscript.

Place	Date	Hour	Summary of Events and Information	Remarks and references to Appendices
WESTROVE	29		Baths.	
	30		Route march and Tactical Exercise (Outposts).	
	31		Tactical Scheme (Outposts).	
			CASUALTIES for the month NIL.	

31 July 1917.

Rowley Lieut.
for O.C. 169. Machine Gun Coy.

Confidential

War Diary

of

169th Machine Gun Company

from 1st August 1917   to 31st August 1917

MAPS. HAZEBROUCK 6A EDN. 2.
BELGIUM & SHEET. 27. EDN 2.
FRANCE

Army Form C. 2118

WAR DIARY
or
INTELLIGENCE SUMMARY
(Erase heading not required.)

Instructions regarding War Diaries and Intelligence Summaries are contained in F.S. Regs., Part II. and the Staff Manual respectively. Title Pages will be prepared in manuscript.

AUGUST.

Place	Date	Hour	Summary of Events and Information	Remarks and references to Appendices
WESTROVE. Nr. EPERLECQUES.	1.		The whole Company less Q.M. Stores and a few details proceeded to TOURNEHEM. for the purpose of practising a Machine Gun Demonstration to be held on the 3rd inst.	
TOURNEHEM.	2.		Owing to rain no practice march was held in afternoon.	
	3.		Demonstration was cancelled, a practice machine Gun barrage however took place in the morning. Company marched back to billets at WESTROVE in afternoon.	
WESTROVE.	4.		Gun and equipment cleaning.	
	5.	4 a.m.	All Transport, Nos. 1 and 2 sections, and part of No. 3. Section proceeded by road to NOORDPEENE.	
	6.	7 a.m.	The remainder of Coy. moved with Brigade and marched to ST. OMER. entraining at ST. OMER at 12.40 p.m. and proceeded to HOPOUTRE where Coy. detrained and proceeded to WIPPEN HOEK area. Billeted at K. 35. a. 9. 9 [BELGIUM and FRANCE SHEET. 27.]	
K. 35. a. 9. 9.	7.		Gas Helmet inspection by Commanding Officer.	
	8.		General Machine Gun Training.	

1875 Wt. W593/826 1,000,000 4/15 J.B.C. & A. A.D.S.S./Forms/C. 2118.

MAP. ZILLEBEKE. 1/10.000 Edⁿ 6.A.

WAR DIARY
or
INTELLIGENCE SUMMARY
(Erase heading not required.)

Army Form C. 2118

Instructions regarding War Diaries and Intelligence Summaries are contained in F. S. Regs, Part II. and the Staff Manual respectively. Title Pages will be prepared in manuscript.

Place	Date	Hour	Summary of Events and Information	Remarks and references to Appendices
K.35.a.9.9.	9.		Squad drill. Combined Gun Drill and Gas Drill. The Brigadier General inspected 16 mules with pack- saddling.	
	10.		General M.G. training in forenoon; range practice in afternoon.	
	11.	1:15 p.m.	Transport moved by road to DICKEBUSCH.	
		2:45 p.m.	Coy. marched to REELE and entrained for CHATEAU SEGARD area H.29.b.9.6. bivouacking in the open.	
H.29.b.9.6	12	2 p.m.	Coy. moved into line in ZILLEBEKE SECTOR, transport remaining at DICKEBUSCH. Coy. relieved 53rd M.G. Coy. Coy. H.Q. in MAPLE TRENCH. at I.24.a.2.4. with Advanced H.Q. in TUNNEL at J.13.b.4.1.	
			Disposition of guns.	
			Sect. 1. 4 guns in reserve at MAPLE TRENCH.	
			Sect. 2. 3 guns in reserve at TUNNEL.	
			1 gun in position outside TUNNEL at J.13.b.3.2.	
			Sect. 3. 4 guns in reserve at MAPLE TRENCH.	
			Sect. 4. 2 guns in STRONG POINT J.14.a.3.2.	
			1 gun at J.13.c.3.7. (SURBITON VILLAS).	
			1 gun at J.8.c.4.1.	

1875 Wt. W593/826 1,000,000 4/15 J.B.C. & A. A.D.S.S./Forms/C. 2118.

Army Form C. 2118

WAR DIARY
or
INTELLIGENCE SUMMARY
(Erase heading not required.)

Place	Date	Hour	Summary of Events and Information	Remarks and references to Appendices
I.24.a.24	13.		Attempt by Q.V.R. and Q.W.R. to form advanced posts. No. M.G. firing.	
	14.		1 gun, No. 4. Sect. at STRONG POINT put out of action by shell fire, but replaced by 1 gun of No. 2. Sect. 4 guns positions in SANCTUARY WOOD extending from J.13.c.45.70 to J.13.c.45.85 prepared by Sect. 3. ready for barrage fire.	
		8.30 p.m.	Heavy enemy artillery barrage on lower edge of SANCTUARY WOOD.	
J.13.b.4.1.	15		Coy H.Q. removed to TUNNEL at J.13.b.4.1. Section 1. went to Assembly Trenches ready for attack distribution of guns being :- 2 guns with 1/2nd LONDON REGT. 2 guns with 1/5th LONDON REGT.	
	16	4.45 a.m.	"Zero" hour. Work accomplished by sections was as follows:- Sect.1. 2 guns with 1/2nd LONDON REGT. only able to advance as far as STRONG POINT J.14.d.3.2. 2 guns with 1/5th LONDON REGT. forced to retire to TUNNEL. Sect. 2. 3 guns in reserve at in TUNNEL ready to proceed to POLYGONE WOOD if possible. 1 gun brought down enemy aeroplane at 10 a.m. in neighbourhood of Coy. H.Q.	

WAR DIARY
or
INTELLIGENCE SUMMARY
(Erase heading not required.)

Army Form C. 2118

Place	Date	Hour	Summary of Events and Information	Remarks and references to Appendices
T.13.b.4.1.	16.		Section 3. Barrage fire from positions ranging from T.13.c.45.40 to T.13.c.45.80. Targets for first barrage. T.13.d.5.1. to T.20.b.5.4. " " second " T.21.a.0.9. to T.20.b.85.45. Clearance of crest tested by Tangent sight and found sufficient for safety of Troops there. During the firing an Officer of the Company reported bullets going well over and giving Infantry great confidence. Rounds fired ---- 11,500. Section 4. 1 gun at STRONG POINT. put out of action by M.G. fire, but replaced later by 1 gun of No.1. section.	
T.24.a.24	17.	5.15 to 7 p.m.	Coy. H.Q. removed to MAPLE TRENCH. at T.24.a.2.4. Neighbourhood of Coy. H.Q. heavily bombarded by enemy artillery searching for our artillery batteries. 2 guns Section 3. relieved 2 guns Section 4 in STRONG POINT. 2 guns Section 2. relieved 2 guns Section 4 at T.8.C.4.1 and T.13.c.3.7.	
	18.		Coy relieved by teams of 41st. and 42nd. M.G. Companies. Sections marched independently to Transport lines at DICKEBUSCH.	

WAR DIARY
or
INTELLIGENCE SUMMARY
(Erase heading not required.)

Army Form C. 2118

Instructions regarding War Diaries and Intelligence Summaries are contained in F.S. Regs., Part II. and the Staff Manual respectively. Title Pages will be prepared in manuscript.

Place	Date	Hour	Summary of Events and Information	Remarks and references to Appendices
DICKEBUSCH.	19.		Coy. moved by motor lorry, Transport by road to WIPPENHOEK area.	
K.35.a.9.9.	20.		Gun and equipment cleaning. Coy. H.Q. at K.35.a.9.9.	
	21.		Limber cleaning and painting.	
	22.		Packing limbers and general training.	
	23.		Transport moved by road to ARNEKE.	
	24.		Transport moved by road from ARNEKE to SALPERWICK. Coy. entrained at ABEELE for WATTEN and marched to SALPERWICK.	
SALPERWICK.	25.		Coy. H.Q. at R.21.c.0.4. Gun cleaning, belt filling, and squad drill.	
	26.		Church Parade.	
	27.		Baths in forenoon, section exercises in afternoon.	
	28.		Advanced M.G. training, Inspection of P.H. helmets and box respirator (half Coy.).	
	29.		Tests of Elementary training, Fire Direction, and Aiming drill. Inspection of P.H. helmets and box respirator (half Coy.).	

MAP. LENS 11.

Army Form C. 2118

WAR DIARY
or
INTELLIGENCE SUMMARY
(Erase heading not required.)

Instructions regarding War Diaries and Intelligence Summaries are contained in F. S. Regs., Part II. and the Staff Manual respectively. Title Pages will be prepared in manuscript.

Place	Date	Hour	Summary of Events and Information	Remarks and references to Appendices
SALPERWICK	30.	7 p.m.	Coy. marched to WIZERNES.	
		11.34 p.m.	Coy. entrained at WIZERNES for MIRAUMONT.	
MIRAUMONT.	31.		Coy. marched from MIRAUMONT to neighbourhood of BANCOURT. Coy. H.Q. - South of road under second I in Tordoir (MAP. LENS 11).	
			TOTAL CASUALTIES FOR MONTH. 5. O.R. KILLED 21. O.R. WOUNDED 3. O.R. MISSING.	

1/9/17.

[Stamp: No. 169 MACHINE GUN COMPANY. No. OR. 523.]

R. [signature] Lt.
for O.C. 169 Machine Gun Coy.

Vol 15

Confidential

War Diary

of

169th Machine Gun Company

from 1st September 1917   to 30th September 1917

Army Form C. 2118

MAPS 57.c.
57.c.N.E.

WAR DIARY
or
INTELLIGENCE SUMMARY
(Erase heading not required.)

SEPTEMBER

Instructions regarding War Diaries and Intelligence Summaries are contained in F. S. Regs., Part II. and the Staff Manual respectively. Title Pages will be prepared in manuscript.

Place	Date	Hour	Summary of Events and Information	Remarks and references to Appendices
BARICOURT H.36.c.o.7.	1.		Machine Gun Training under Section Officers.	
	2.		Church Parade.	
	3.		Baths.	

	4.		Cleaning and packing limbers, and cleaning of Camp Area. Company relieved 8th. M.G.Coy. in line, in LOUVERVAL Sector. Sections 1 & 4 in reserve at Transport lines at I.29.a.2.1. Company H.Q. at J.20.c.85.90.
			
			Disposition of guns.
			  Left Section. (No 2). Right Section. (No 3).
			  Section H.Q.: J.4.c.6.9. Section H.Q. J.16.b.50.98.
			             J.6.a.1.2. J.12.d.1.5.
			             D.29.c.1.4. J.16.b.50.98.
			             J.10.b.05.80. J.17.b.5.5.
			             J.4.c.75.60. J.10.c.7.5.	

J.20.c.85.90	5.		Situation quiet. Work on shelters for teams continued and emplacements strengthened.	
	6.		Gun at J.6.a.1.2. fired between 1 a.m. and 4 a.m. on Listening Posts in E.26.c. and on work at E.25.b.2.5. 1,000 rounds expended.	
	7.		Enemy active with "whizz bangs" on left of LOUVERVAL. Small numbers of enemy observed on ridge at D.24.b. Enemy Machine Guns active during night.	
	8.		Day and night quiet. Enemy shelled left of BOURSIES with "whizz bangs" at intervals during night. General work of construction of positions continued.	
	9.		Day and night quiet. Work continued. Enemy dropped a few shells in valley at D.29.c.3.8.	

1875 Wt. W593/826 1,000,000 4/15 J.B.C. & A. A.D.S.S./Forms/C. 2118.

Army Form C. 2118.

WAR DIARY
or
INTELLIGENCE SUMMARY.
(Erase heading not required.)

Instructions regarding War Diaries and Intelligence Summaries are contained in F. S. Regs., Part II. and the Staff Manual respectively. Title pages will be prepared in manuscript.

Place	Date	Hour	Summary of Events and Information	Remarks and references to Appendices
J.20.c.85.90.	10/11		Day and night quiet. Work continued.	
	12.		Enemy aircraft action. Machine flying low was engaged by our guns and driven off. Rounds fired: 300. Enemy Machine Guns fairly active at night. Work continued on shelters and emplacements. Nos. 1 & 4 Sections relieved Nos. 2 & 3 Sections in the line.	
	13.		Front quiet. Day and night shifts employed on work in progress, mainly saps, dugouts, and emplacements.	
	14.		Left section H.Q. removed to J.10.b.05.80.	
	15.		Quiet. A great deal of movement observed in enemy lines and duly reported. General work continued. Right Section H.Q. removed to J.10.d.45.05.	
	16.		Day and night quiet.	
	17.		Slight increase in enemy artillery activity. Work continued on dugouts, emplacements, saps, and shelters.	
	18.		Situation quiet.	
	19.		Night exceptionally quiet.	
	20.		Between 2.25 p.m. and 3.50 p.m. about 30 shells (H.E. & Shrapnel) were fired at and over the trench running from J.5. Infantry Post to gully. Remainder of 24 hrs. normal. Nos. 2 & 3 Sections relieved Nos. 1 & 4 Sections in the line.	
	21.		Gun team from J.17.b.5.6. removed to J.17.d.3.7., the former ceasing to be an occupied position.	

Army Form C. 2118.

WAR DIARY
or
INTELLIGENCE SUMMARY.
(Erase heading not required.)

Instructions regarding War Diaries and Intelligence
Summaries are contained in F. S. Regs., Part II.
and the Staff Manual respectively. Title pages
will be prepared in manuscript.

Place	Date	Hour	Summary of Events and Information	Remarks and references to Appendices
J.10.c.45.90	22.		Enemy artillery active on BOURSIES. Good progress made on dugout at J.10.b.05.80. and on tunnel at J.16.b.50.98.	
	23		Situation normal. Thick mist prevented much observation.	
	24.		Enemy aeroplane flew over at low altitude in pursuit of one of ours. Two guns opened fire but without result. Rounds fired: 500. Gun at J.6.a.1.2. fired on supposed enemy M.G. emplacement at E.19.a.3.3. and on E.19.cent. where movement had been observed. Rounds fired: 500.	
	25.		Enemy artillery more active than usual, 20 shells (4.2) falling in valley to right of gun at J.6.a.1.2. Gun at J.4.c.75.60. fired 1,000 rounds at enemy aircraft during the day.	
	26.		Gun at J.12.d.1.b. carried out searching fire from 11.30 p.m. to 3 a.m. between K.1.b.95.90. and J.1.b.8.0. Road from K.1.b.8.0. to Crater also traversed. Rounds fired: 2,000.	
	27.		" At request of Infantry, gun at J.4.c.75.60. laid to cover left flank of post along INCHY ROAD. Dugout at J.10.b.05.80 completed, and good progress made on tunnel at J.16.b.50.98.	
	28.		Nos. 1 & 4 Sections relieved Nos. 2 & 3 Sections in the line. Situation quiet.	
	29.		Heavy mist during night and early forenoon, preventing much observation.	
	30.		Situation quiet.	

Casualties for the month. Nil.

O.C. 169. Machine Gun Company.

[Signature] Lieut.
Machine Gun Company.

Vol. 16

Confidential

War Diary

of

169th Machine Gun Company

from 1st October 1917   To 31st October 1917

MAPS. 57.c.
57.c.N.E.

WAR DIARY
or
INTELLIGENCE SUMMARY.
(Erase heading not required.)

OCTOBER 1917.

Army Form C. 2118.

Place	Date	Hour	Summary of Events and Information	Remarks and references to Appendices
J.20.c.8.9.	1.		Great increase in enemy artillery activity, several shells falling in vicinity of gun position at J.13.d.1.5. but no damage done.	
	2.	10 p.m.	Situation quiet during fore-noon. Good progress made on work in hand. Hostile aeroplane passed over BEAUMETZ, intermediate line, and after circling village of LOUVERVAL returned to enemy lines.	
	3.		Increase in enemy artillery activity during early morning hours, dying down at dawn.	
	4.		Situation quiet.	
	5.		Day and night quiet. Gun at J.13.d.1.5. fired on target from K.2.c.50.55. to K.2.a.6.3. Rounds fired: 1500. Nos. 2 and 3 Sections relieved Nos. 1 and 4 Sections in the Line.	
	6.		Quiet. Good progress made on dugout at J.10.b.05.80. and tunnel at J.16.b.50.98.	
	7.		Situation normal.	
	8.		Enemy artillery more active. DOIGNIES shelled from 12 noon to 7 p.m. a few shells falling near Section H.Q. at J.16.b.50.98. Gun at J.13.d.1.5. fired 500 rounds on Listening post in E.26.c. between 4 a.m. and 6 a.m. and gun at J.13.d.1.5. fired 1500 rounds on enemy's new line and CAMBRAI ROAD from K.1.b.9.9. to K.1.b.9.2.	
	9.		Quiet. Work on dugouts, tunnel, and shelters progressing well.	
	10.		Quiet. Occasional shells near J.16.b.50.98. from 7.30 p.m. to 10.30 p.m.	
	11.		Enemy artillery active during night. LOUVERVAL shelled with shrapnel between 9.30 p.m. and 11 p.m. Fairly heavy shelling in vicinity of position at J.6.a.1.2.	

Army Form C. 2118.

WAR DIARY
or
INTELLIGENCE SUMMARY.
(Erase heading not required.)

Instructions regarding War Diaries and Intelligence Summaries are contained in F. S. Regs., Part II. and the Staff Manual respectively. Title pages will be prepared in manuscript.

Place	Date	Hour	Summary of Events and Information	Remarks and references to Appendices
J.20.c.8.9.	12.		Day and night quiet.	
	13.		Between 60 and 80 77mm. shells fell on INCHY ROAD between J.4.b.5.5. and LOUVERVAL. Gun at D.29.c.1.4. fired 800 rounds on E.19.c.7.1. from 8 p.m. to 10p.m. No. 1 Section relieved No. 3 Section in line.	
	14.		Situation very quiet. No. 1 Section relieved No. 2 Section in line.	
	15.	9 p.m.	Gun at J.12.d.1.5. fired 500 rounds on barrage lines from 7.15 p.m. to	
	16.		2 Shells (5.9) fell in DOIGNIES at 2.5. p.m.	
	17.	11.45 a.m.	Aerial activity above normal in early morning. Enemy working party at D.30.central. dispersed by fire from gun taken from J.6.a.1.2. into gully on right of position. 250 rounds expended.	
	18.		Artillery of both sides more active. British plane crashed in aerial combat, falling at D.30.a.7.2. 6 "whizz bangs fell 30 yds. north of gun osition at J.12.d.1.5. and 4 shells (5.9) about J.12.d.2.3.	
	19.		Situation quiet. Good progress made with works under construction.	
	20.		Enemy artillery more active.	
	21/22		Situation quiet.	
	23.	11 p.m. and 12 midnight.	Vicinity of Section H.Q. at J.16.b.50.98. shelled with 4.2 shells between One direct hit made on trench but little damage done Relieved Sections 2 and 3 relieved Sections 1 and 4 in the line.	
	24.	10.45 p.m.	Gun at J.1.2.d.1.5. fired on CRATER at K.2.a.10.75. from 10 p.m. to Rounds expended: 500.	

Army Form C. 2118.

WAR DIARY
or
INTELLIGENCE SUMMARY.
(Erase heading not required.)

Instructions regarding War Diaries and Intelligence Summaries are contained in F. S. Regs., Part II. and the Staff Manual respectively. Title pages will be prepared in manuscript.

Place	Date	Hour	Summary of Events and Information	Remarks and references to Appendices
J.20.c.8.9.	25		Situation quiet. 2 guns at J.12.b.1.2. fired on CAMBRAI ROAD in E.26.d. Rounds expended: 500 at 12 midnight, 1500 from 4 a.m. to 6 a.m.	
	26.		Situation normal.	
	27.		DOIGNIES shelled persistently throughout the day with shells of heavy calibre.	
	28.		Situation quiet.	
	29.		Enemy artillery active. Neighbourhood of BEETROOT FACTORY at J.9.b.4.3. shelled during the day with 4.2 and 5.9 shells. Hostile plane flying low, fired on party working in SPRAT TRENCH. Sunken Road between Cemetery and Crucifix in J.12. shelled from 8 p.m. to 2 a.m. with 77 mm. and 4.2 shells. Nos. 1 and 4 Sections relieved Nos. 2 and 3 Sections in the line.	
	30.		Cross Roads at J.9.b.6.3. shelled between 8.30 p.m. and 9 p.m. and between 9.30 p.m. and 10 p.m. DOIGNIES shelled with 5.9s between 9 p.m. and 11 p.m.	
	31.		Situation normal.	
			CASUALTIES during month. Nil.	
			The following captured trophies have now been recorded to the Company. Machine Guns: Nos. 7542. 1072A. 8137. Machine Gun Mounting. No number. Authority:- W.O. 57/8/39 (A3) dated 20/9/17. W.O. 57/8/9897 (A3) dated 18/9/17.	

O.C. 169. Machine Gun Company.

Major.

CONFIDENTIAL

WAR DIARY

169th M.G Coy.

NOVEMBER 1917

Confidential

MAPS. FRANCE
57.c
5y.c N.E.

WAR DIARY
or
INTELLIGENCE SUMMARY.
(Erase heading not required.)

NOVEMBER 1917.

Army Form C. 2118.

Instructions regarding War Diaries and Intelligence Summaries are contained in F. S. Regs. Part II. and the Staff Manual respectively. Title pages will be prepared in manuscript.

Place	Date	Hour	Summary of Events and Information	Remarks and references to Appendices
J.20.c.8.9.	1		Gun at J.12.d.1.5. fired on K.3.a. and K.3.c. from 11 p.m. to 1 a.m. 1500 rounds expended.	
	2		Situation quiet.	
	3		Hostile shelling on DOIGNIES-BOURSIES Road and on O.P. on DOIGNI S&D MICOURT Road between 5.30 p.m. and 8.15 p.m. with 4.2 and 77 mm. shells.	
	4		Situation quiet.	
	5		vicinity of Section H.Q. at J.10.b.05.80. shelled with 4.2 and 77 mm. shells 1 direct hit being obtained on dugout; no damage done.	
	6		Situation very quiet.	
	7		Nos. 2 and 3 Sections relieved Nos. 1 and 4 Sections in the line, relief complete at 7.44 p.m.	
	8/14		Situation very quiet. Work on Battery Positions and S.A.A. dumps established in preparation for forthcoming operations.	
	15		Nos. 1 and 4 Sections relieved Nos. 2 and 3 Sections in the line, relief complete at 7.30 p.m.	
	16/18		Situation very quiet.	
	19		Company H.Q. removed to J.16.b.50.98.	
J.16.b.50.98.	20.		Zero Hour 6.20 a.m. In cooperation with the Infantry in the feint attack 4 guns of No. 4 Section fired 12,000 rounds from Zero to Zero plus 15 minutes 2 guns firing on the BARRICAD on the BAPAUME - CAMBRAI RD. at K.1.b.85.55. and 2 guns on target K.8.a.4.9. 50 of the enemy were seen to run away from trench at K.8.a.6.7. as a result of fire upon K.8.a.4.9. Observation was rendered very difficult owing to smoke barrage and mist.	

WAR DIARY or INTELLIGENCE SUMMARY.

(Erase heading not required.)

Army Form C. 2118.

Place	Date	Hour	Summary of Events and Information	Remarks and references to Appendices
J.16.b.50.98	20		Section 3 formed "D" Battery working under the orders of the D.M.G.O. A Battery line of 8 guns was established at K.V.d.3.5. and the following barrages carried out. "A". Bridge at Crossing of CANAL DU NORD over RAPAUME - CAMBRAI RD. (E.27.c.1.4.) from Zero to Zero plus 300 minutes. Rate of fire: 50 rounds per minute. Rounds expended: 60,000. "B". Barrage Line K.2.b.5.4. to K.2.a.2.9. from Zero plus 322 to Zero plus 332 minutes. Rate of fire: 50 rounds per minute. Rounds expended: 4,500. "C". Barrage Line K.2.a.60.95. to E.27.3.0. from Zero plus 232 to Zero plus 342 minutes. Rate of fire: 50 rounds per minute. Rounds expended: 3,500. "D". Barrage Line E.36.c.0.4. to W.36.d.8.9. from Zero plus 342 to Zero plus 392 minutes. Rate of fire: 50 rounds per minute. Rounds expended: 7,000.	
	21		Infantry went over at 11 a.m. and established themselves in TADPOLE COPSE. 2 teams of No. 4 Section moved to FISH ALLY for purpose of firing on HINDENBURG LINE in event of S.O.S. call.	
	22		No. 1 Section moved forward to the following positions:- 1 gun at J.6.a.15.40. 1 gun at J.5.b.5.5. 1 gun at J.5.b.3.6. 1 gun at D.29.d.1.2. No. 4 Section moved forward to the following positions:- 2 guns at D.24.b.7.4. 1 gun at 1.35.b.10.4. 1 gun at 118.a.35.00. No. 3 Section in support at Left Section H.Q. at J.10.b.05.80.	
	23		1 gun of No. 4 Section moved to the CRATER at D.24.a.6.6. and No. 4 Section H.Q. to German dugout at D.24.b.8.4. The old German outpost line was subjected to heavy shelling during the afternoon, and the following Casualties occurred: 1 O.R. killed, 3 O.R. wounded. During the counter attack on the LONDON SCOTTISH, the guns of No. 4	
	24		Section fired 2,000 rounds to prevent the enemy attacking and bombing over the top.	

Army Form C. 2118.

WAR DIARY
or
INTELLIGENCE SUMMARY.
(Erase heading not required.)

Place	Date	Hour	Summary of Events and Information	Remarks and references to Appendices
J.16.d.50.98	25		Gun at CRATER, D.3.a.6.6. withdrawn to Right Section H.Q. DOIGNIES. No. 4 Section's guns fired during the afternoon, supporting the attack delivered by the 168. Infantry Brigade. No. 2 Section relieved No. 4 Section in the line.	
	26		Disposition of guns at nightfall was as follows:- 2 guns at E.26.a.1.1. 2 guns at E.25.b.7.4. "A.A." 1 gun at D.24.b.8.4. 1 gun at J.6.a.15.40. 1 gun at J.5.b.5.5. "A.A." 1 gun at J.5.b.2.8. 1 gun at D.29.d.1.3. 3 guns at J.10.d.5.0. (Coy. H.Q.)	
	27		The S.O.S. was observed at 3.20 p.m. in direction of TADPOLE COPSE. Our guns in the line opened fire on their S.O.S. lines, and some of the enemy who had previously left their trenches in E.13.d. were seen to retire hurriedly. Rounds fired:- 6,000.	
	28		3 guns of No. 1 Section relieved 3 guns of No. 2 Section in the line, the latter then occupying the positions vacated by No. 1 Section in the British old Front Line, with H.Q. in WHITING. 2 guns of No. 4 Section relieved the other 2 guns of that Section.	
	29		Enemy artillery active in shelling back areas, mainly DEMICOURT-MOEUVRES ROAD and MOEUVRES reserve trench.	
	30.		4 guns at E.25.b. fired 18,000 rounds, and gun at D.24.b.8.4. 2,350 rounds on S.O.S. lines between 10.15 a.m. and 3 p.m. during enemy attack. Disposition of guns at 6 p.m. 1 gun at D.24.b.8.4. 1 gun in E.25.a. 4 guns from E.25.b.7.4. 6 guns in old British Front Line in to E.25.b.8.3. J.6.b. CASUALTIES for the month:- 1 O.R. killed. 3 O.R. wounded. O.C. 169. Machine Gun Company. 1/12/17. Major.	

35807. W16879/M1879 500,000 3/17 R.T. (1074) Forms/W3091/3

Army Form W.3091.

9/4/18

Cover for Documents.

Nature of Enclosures.

CONFIDENTIAL

WAR DIARY

169TH MACHINE GUN COMPANY.

DECEMBER 1917.

Notes, or Letters written.

Maps: 57.c. N.E.
51.B. N.W.

Army Form C. 2118.

WAR DIARY
or
INTELLIGENCE SUMMARY.
(Erase heading not required.)

Instructions regarding War Diaries and Intelligence Summaries are contained in F.S. Regs., Part II. and the Staff Manual respectively. Title pages will be prepared in manuscript.

Place	Date	Hour	Summary of Events and Information	Remarks and references to Appendices
T.20.c.8.9 (57C.N.E)	1		Gun at D.24.b.6.4. fired 2,250 rounds on S.O.S. lines.	
	2		154 M.G. Coy. relieved this Company in the line, the Numbers 1 of each gun remaining for 24 hours to hand over orders and instructions. The rest of the Company proceeded to Company Transport Lines at LEBUCQUIERE.	
LEBUCQUIERE	3.		Company marched to PREMICOURT, entraining there for BEAUMETZ LES LOGES, and then proceeded to BERNEVILLE by road.	
BERNEVILLE	4		Gun and equipment cleaning.	
ANZIN ST AUBIN	5		Company marched to ANZIN ST AUBIN via WARLUS - DUISANS - MAROEUIL.	
	6		Cleaning of guns and equipment and testing and tuning up of guns on range.	
B.26.7.85.30. (51.B.N.W)	7		Company proceeded to GAVRELLE AREA. Coy. H.Q. at B.26.c.85.30. 2 guns of No. 2 Section relieved of 92 M.G.Coy. at H.6.b.18.50. 4 guns of No. 2 Section and 2 guns of No. 2 Section relieved 6 guns of 92 M.G. Coy. at THAMES BATTERY (B.30.a.12.75.) 3 guns of No. 1 Section relieved of 242 M.G. Coy., 3 guns at B.29.a.1.7. 1 gun at H.5.a.8.4. Remaining 5 guns in reserve at ROPER'S CAMP.	
	8		2 guns at H.6.b.18.50. moved to H.6.a.4.8.	
	9		Situation quiet.	
	10.		3 guns of the 5 in reserve at ROPER'S CAMP took up positions as follows: B.28.d.60.85. H.5.a.55.65.	
	11		1gun of 168 M.G. Coy. relieved 1 gun of No. 1 Section at B.29.a.1.7. Considerable enemy aerial activity.	
			Quiet.	

WAR DIARY
or
INTELLIGENCE SUMMARY.
(Erase heading not required.)

Army Form C. 2118.

Place	Date	Hour	Summary of Events and Information	Remarks and references to Appendices
B.26.T.85.30	12/15		Situation normal.	
	16		A 5.9 shell fell on entrance to dugout at THAMES BATTERY, wounding 1 O.R. standing near by. Inter Section relief at THAMES BATTERY.	
	17		Situation quiet.	
	18	7-11 p.m.	Spasmodic M.G. fire in neighbourhood of THAMES BATTERY.	
	19		Situation normal.	
	20		Situation very quiet.	
	21		Good progress made with improvements to shelters and trenches at all gun positions during the past week.	
	22		4 guns in RED LINE relieved by 4 guns of 193 M.G. Coy. 1 O.R. killed	
	23	5-11 p.m.	Guns fired 4,500 rounds harassing area between C.26.a.cent. & C.25.a.5.2. Inter section relief.	
	24/25	dusk-8p.m. 5-7 a.m.	Guns fired 3,000 rounds harassing track in T.2.a.	
	25/26	6-9 p.m. 5-7 a.m.	Guns fired 6,000 rounds on tracks, road, and trenches at C.25.b.5.3. & T.2.a.	
	26/27	8-10.20 p.m. 4.30-6 a.m.	3,000 rounds fired on tracks and centre of activity at T.26.c.65.10. and T.2.a.70.95. and C.26.a.	
	27	5-7 p.m. 10-11.30 p.m.	3,000 rounds fired harassing centre of activity, trenches and tracks at C.26.b.5.3. and C.26.a. and C.20.c. & d.	
	28/29		Guns fired 4,500 rounds on centres of activity, tracks, and trenches at C.26.b.3. C.25.B.5.6.T.2.C. C.20.C. & d.	

Army Form C. 2118.

WAR DIARY
or
INTELLIGENCE SUMMARY.
(Erase heading not required.)

Instructions regarding War Diaries and Intelligence Summaries are contained in F. S. Regs., Part II. and the Staff Manual respectively. Title pages will be prepared in manuscript.

Place	Date	Hour	Summary of Events and Information	Remarks and references to Appendices
	29/29	7-9.30 p.m. 5.30-7 a.m.	Inter Section relief at THAMES BATTERY. 40 5.9 shells and 4.2 shrapnel fell in the neighbourhood of Coy. H.Q. at R.26.b.6.8.from 2 - 5 p.m. 28th.	
	29/30	10-12 a.m. 5-6.30 a.m.	4,500 rounds fired in harassing tracks at C.26.b.5.2. and on 7.19.d.5.4. and C.20.a.9.2.	
	30/31	5-7 p.m. 10-11.30 p.m.	3,000 rounds fired harassing roads, tracks, and trenches at T.2.a., C.26.a and C.20.c & d.	
	31/1.	7-9.20 p.m. 5-7 a.m.	3,000 rounds fired on tracks around H.Qs. at C.26.c.65.10 and I.2.a.70.95. and on centre of activity at C.26.b.5.3. and trenches in neighbourhood	O.C. 169 Machine Gun Company
			Total number of rounds fired during the month. 37,750.	
			Casualties during the month. 1 O.R. killed. 1 O.R. wounded.	

35807. W16879/M1879 500,000 3/17 R.T. (1074) Forms/W3091/3 Army Form W.3091.

96/19

Cover for Documents.

Nature of Enclosures.

Confidential

War Diary

of

169th Machine Gun Company

for month of

January 1918

Notes, or Letters written.

MAPS. 51 B NW.
FRANCE 56 B.

Army Form C. 2118.

WAR DIARY
or
INTELLIGENCE SUMMARY.
(Erase heading not required.)

JANUARY 1918

Place	Date	Hour	Summary of Events and Information	Remarks and references to Appendices
B.26.A.8.3	1/2		3,000 rounds fired on Centre of activity at C.26.b.5.3.and trenches in neighbourhood and on Centre of Activity in C.26.a. from 6 - 9 p.m. and 5.30 - 6.30 a.m.	
	2/3		3,000 rounds fired on Tracks in C.26.d. and in enfilading tracks immediately N. of GAVRELLE ROAD in C.26.a. and C.20.c.& d. from 8 - 10 p.m. and 5 - 6.30 a.m.	
	3/4		3,000 rounds fired on Tracks leading from H.Qs. at C.26.b.5.3.to CHINK and CHAFF trenches, and on road and trenches in 1.2.a.from 6 - 9 p.m. and 5-7a.m.	
	4		Company was relieved by 168.M.G.Coy.in forenoon and proceeded to ANZIN ST. AUBIN.	
ANZIN ST AUBIN.	5		Company entrained at MAROEUIL for SAVY, from thence proceeding by road to la COMTE.	
la COMTE.	6		Gun and equipment cleaning.	
	7		Gun and equipment cleaning and reorganization of sections.	
	8		General M.G. training under section officers.	
	9		Company engaged in clearing away drifts of snow from road between la COMTE and HERMIN.	
	10		General M.G.training.	
	11		Route march - la COMTE - HOUDAIN - RANCHICOURT - la COMTE.	
	12		Indirect fire exercise on training area.	
	13		Church parades.	
	14		Squad and saluting drill. Immediate action.	

Army Form C. 2118.

WAR DIARY
or
INTELLIGENCE SUMMARY.
(Erase heading not required)

Instructions regarding War Diaries and Intelligence Summaries are contained in F. S. Regs., Part II. and the Staff Manual respectively. Title pages will be prepared in manuscript.

January 1918

Place	Date	Hour	Summary of Events and Information	Remarks and references to Appendices
La Comte.	15		Indirect rire exercise on training area.	
	16		Inspection or box respirators and gas helmets.	
	17		Training under sectional arrangements.	
	18		Route march - la COMTE - crossroads in P.9.b. and P.3.cent. - BEUGIN-laCOMTE.	
	19		Squad drill and indirect rire exercise.	
	20		Church parade.	
	21		Company drill, tests of elementary training and saluting drill.	
	22		Squad drill and general company training. Belt filling in preparation for range practice.	
	23		2 sections cooperated in tactical scheme with the 1/2nd London BRegt.	
			1 " " " " " " 1/9th " "	
	24		2 sections cooperated in tactical scheme with the 1/2nd London Regt. where 1 company Infantry attack M.G. in defensive positions.	
	25		1 section cooperated in tactical scheme with 1/9th London Regt.	
			1 " " " " " " 1/2nd " "	
			2 sections on range.	
	26		General company training - squad drill etc.	
	27		Church parade.	
	28		Range practice, company and pack-saddlery drill.	

Army Form C. 2118.

WAR DIARY
or
INTELLIGENCE SUMMARY.

(Erase heading not required.)

JANUARY 1918

Place	Date	Hour	Summary of Events and Information	Remarks and references to Appendices
La Comte	29		1 section cooperated in tactical scheme with 1/2nd London Regt.	
			1 " " on range practice.	
			2 " " baths and company drill.	
	30		1 section range practice.	
			3 " " general company training.	
	31		3 sections on general offensive and defensive tactical scheme.	
			1 " " company training.	
			Casualties for the month = NIL.	
			Honours and Rewards during the month:—	
			1. Military Cross.	
			2. Military Medals.	
			1. Meritorious Service Medal.	

J Mackie Captain.
O.C. 69 Machine Gun Coy.

9/L-20

35807. W15879/M1879 500,000 3/17 R.T. (1074) Forms/W3091/3

Army Form W.3091.

Cover for Documents.

SECRET

Nature of Enclosures.

WAR DIARY

169TH MACHINE GUN COMPANY

FEBRUARY 1918.

Notes, or Letters written.

Army Form C. 2118.

MAP. FRANCE 51B.
36 A.

WAR DIARY
or
INTELLIGENCE SUMMARY.
(Erase heading not required.)

FEBRUARY 1916.

Instructions regarding War Diaries and Intelligence Summaries are contained in F.S. Regs., Part II. and the Staff Manual respectively. Title pages will be prepared in manuscript.

Place	Date	Hour	Summary of Events and Information	Remarks and references to Appendices
LA COMTE.	1.		Route march	
	2.		Company engaged on tactical scheme attacking and defending a wood and providing a covering party.	
	3.		Church parade.	
	4.		Squad drill, belt filling, overhauling gun equipment and cleaning limbers	
	5.		Revolver practice on range, squad and saluting drill, indication and recognition of targets.	
	6.		Company proceeded to ANZIN ST AUBIN by motor lorry.	
ANZIN.	7.		Company relieved 213 Th. Machine Gun Coy. in line, taking over dispositions as follows	

(a) RIGHT GROUP.
Section H.Q. B.6.a. 55.90.
BIRMINGHAM. H.6.a. 55.86.
BOSTON. B.30.c. 6.1.
BRADFIELD. B.30.c. 5.7.
2 teams accommodated at Sect. H.Q. in readiness to occupy in event of attack
RESERVE 1. H.5.b. 90.55
" 4. B.29.d. 45.45

(b) CENTRE GROUP.
Section H.Q. B.30.a.2.6.
THAMES BATTERY. R. B.30.a.2.6
" " Cent. L. " "
BARNSTAPLE B.30.a.55.65.
2 teams accommodated at THAMES BTY. to occupy in case of attack
RESERVE 6. B.29.b. 45.45
" 1R. B.29.c. 45.95.

c. LEFT GROUP.
Section H.Q. B. 24.d. 2.9.
BURNLEY B. 24.d. 25.40
BELTON. B. 24.d. 2.4
BURTON B. 24.d. 2.9.
2 teams accommodated at Coy. H.Q. (H.1.d.4.5) to occupy in event of attack
RESERVE Y. H.4.d. 25.40
" 6. H.4.d. 15.45

Army Form C. 2118.

WAR DIARY
or
INTELLIGENCE SUMMARY.
(Erase heading not required.)

MAP. FRANCE 51.B.

FEBRUARY 1918.

Place	Date	Hour	Summary of Events and Information	Remarks and references to Appendices
H.1.d.4.5.	8.		Situation quiet. Hostile artillery and M.G's normal. Work on trench in-prov'mts.	
	9.	6.30 to 8.30 p.m.	2,000 rounds fired on tracks in C.26.d., H.Q. and tracks in C.26.c.50.45. BURTON shelled with poison shell five times during night, gas helmets having to be worn.	
	10.	5-6 a.m. 7-7.45 p.m.	2000 rounds fired on tracks in C.26.a. and C.26.c. and B.26.a.	
	11.	6.30 – 8 p.m.	2000 rounds fired on tracks N. of GAVRELLE ROAD in C.20.c. and d, and tracks and trenches in C.26.c. and I.2.a. 5.9 shells fell in neighbourhood of BURNLEY and BURTON during the night. BURTON received special attention between 11.30 p.m. and 1 a.m., 25 shells falling very near.	
	12.	6.30 – 8 p.m.	2000 rounds fired on tracks and trenches in C.26.c. and I.2.a. and on road from C.20.c.2.4. to C.20.c.8.9.	
	13.		Three guns of 164 M.G. Coy. relieved 3 guns of No. 3 Section, 1 gun of which relieved gun of No. 2 Section at BRADFIELD.	
		6.15 to 7 p.m.	750 rounds fired on H.Q. and tracks in C.26.c.50.45.	
	14.	5-6 a.m.	1000 rounds fired on tracks and road in C.20.c. and C.26.a.	
		6.15 to 7.45 p.m.	1000 rounds fired on tracks N. of GAVRELLE RD. in C.20.c and d.	
		8-9 p.m.	1000 rounds fired on tracks in C.26.a.	

Army Form C. 2118.

WAR DIARY
or
INTELLIGENCE SUMMARY.
(Erase heading not required.)

MAP. FRANCE 51 B.

FEBRUARY 1918.

Instructions regarding War Diaries and Intelligence Summaries are contained in F.S. Regs., Part II. and the Staff Manual respectively. Title pages will be prepared in manuscript.

Place	Date	Hour	Summary of Events and Information	Remarks and references to Appendices
H.1.d.4.5	15	6.30 – 8 p.m.	1000 rounds fired on tracks in C.26.a.	
	16	5-6 a.m.	1000 rounds fired on tracks in C.26.a.	
		6.15 to 7 p.m.	" " CHEAPSIDE C.T. in C.26.b.	
		6-7 p.m.	" " Tracks leading from WHINE TR.(C.26.7.5.0), HOLLOW COPSE & SQUAREWOOD.	
		7 p.m.	During the day 250 rounds were fired on hostile aircraft. 3 bombs were dropped by enemy plane near BIRMINGHAM, when gun was firing but no damage was done.	
	17.	6-8 p.m.	1000 rounds fired on tracks and trench in C.26.a & c. 450 rounds on tracks north of GAVRELLE RD. in C.20.c and d, and during the day 500 rounds on E.A.	
	18.		Nos. 2 and 4.D sections relieved No.1 and No.3 sections in the line; No.1 Section proceeded to ST. CATHERINE as Bn. Reserve, and No.1. to Coy. H.Q. as Bde. reserve	
	19	10.30 a.m. to noon	2500 rounds fired on tracks in C.25.b, and on M.G. position at B.29.B.90.25.	
		6.30 to 6.30 p.m.	2500 rounds fired on H.Q and tracks at C.26.c.50.40 and C.26.a.	
			around C.26.c. 15.30.	
	20	6 – 7.45 p.m.	2500 rounds fired on Tracks in C.26.b. and C.26.a.	
	21.	7.30 – 9 p.m.	1500 rounds fired on tracks in C.26.b.	

Army Form C. 2118.

MAP. FRANCE 51B.

WAR DIARY
or
INTELLIGENCE SUMMARY.
(Erase heading not required.)

Instructions regarding War Diaries and Intelligence Summaries are contained in F. S. Regs., Part II. and the Staff Manual respectively. Title pages will be prepared in manuscript.

FEBRUARY 1918.

Place	Date	Hour	Summary of Events and Information	Remarks and references to Appendices
H.1.d.4.5	2/22.		General rearrangement of positions took place, after which dispositions were as follows.	
			Gun No. 1. B. 30. a. 9.8. Gun No. 5. B. 29. d. 6.5.	
			" 2. " " 9. H. 4. d. 2.5	
			" 3. H. 5. a. 55.86. " 10 " H. 3. b. 6.8.	
			" 4. B. 29. b. 40. 35. " 11 H. 3. b. 6.8.	
			" 12 H. 4. a. 1.6.	
	22/23.	11-11.45 pm. 5-5.30 a.m.	1,000 rounds fired on CHEAPSIDE C.T. in C. 26. b.	
			Further positions were occupied as follows:-	
			Gun No. 6. B. 29. d. Y. 3. Gun No. 8. H.5. b. 6.5.	
			" 7. Y. H. 5. b. 6. 4.	
	23.		Inter-section relief	
		6.30 to 8 pm.	1500 rounds fired on tracks in C. 26.a.	
	24.	6.30 to 6.30 pm	1500 rounds fired on tracks north of GAVRELLE ROAD. in C. 20.c. and c.	
		10 to 11.30 pm.	1500 rounds fired on tracks in C. 25. b.	
	25	8-9.30 pm.	1500 rounds fired on centres of activity.	
		6.30 to 8.30 pm.	1500 rounds fired on junction of CHEAPSIDE and GAVRELLE support trenches and in enfilading CHEAPSIDE.	

MAP. FRANCE 51B.

WAR DIARY
or
INTELLIGENCE SUMMARY.

Army Form C. 2118.

FEBRUARY 1918.

Place	Date	Hour	Summary of Events and Information	Remarks and references to Appendices
H.1.d.4.5.	26.	4:30 a.m. to dawn.	1,000 rounds fired on tracks in C.26.a. Inter-section relief.	
	27.		4,000 rounds were expended in enfilading WANT TRENCH (I.1.b) in support of raid by Brigade on our right.	
	28.		Situation quiet.	
			No. of rounds expended during month. 42,250.	
			No. of casualties during month - NIL.	

J. C. L—— Capt.
O.C. 169th Machine Gun Coy.

No. 169 MACHINE GUN COMPANY.
D.72
1/3/18.